SAY "YES" TO LOVE

Giving Birth to a World of Love

THE MESSAGES FROM GOD

Through Yael and Doug Powell

Circle of Light Press

Eureka Springs, Arkansas

Say "Yes" to Love,
Giving Birth to a World of Love
THE MESSAGES FROM GOD
Through Yael and Doug Powell

Copyright 2005 by Yael and Doug Powell

Paperback Original ISBN 0-9725991-5-0
Circle of Light Press

Yael and Doug Powell
Circle of Light Press
3969 Mundell Road
Eureka Springs, AR 72631

Cover illustration and book layout by Judith Bicking
Compilation, editing of Messages by Shanna Mac Lean

Websites: www.circleoflight.net
www.unitingtwinflames.com
www.netoflight.com
Email: connect@circleoflight.net

Printing by InstantPublisher.com Collierville, TN

THE **SAY 'YES' TO LOVE** SERIES
The Messages from God
Through Yael and Doug Powell

On SoulMates (Twin Flames)

Say "Yes" to Love, God Explains SoulMates

*Say "Yes" to Love, God Unveils SoulMate Love
and Sacred Sexuality*

On Christ Consciousness

Say "Yes" to Love, God's Guidance to LightWorkers

*Say "Yes" to Love, God Leads Humanity
Toward Christ Consciousness*

*Say "Yes" to Love, Giving Birth to
A World of Love*

On Animal Communication

*Say "Yes" to Love, Magic Cat (an enlightened
animal) Explains Creation*

Words from Our Readers

How can I express through the mediocre means of verbiage what my heart has garnered from the *Messages from God?* Step by loving step, the lessons provided have gently guided me to a remembrance of how to create from pure love; allowing God to live and love through me beyond the limitations of ego. These profound communications, so passionately, consistently, and selflessly provided through the Circle of Light, have kept my heart on course as it has opened into unimaginable vistas of beauty and ecstasy. Without reservation, I claim this as the most critically important information flooding the consciousness of mankind today! Angelina Heart, author of *The Teaching of Little Crow*, Virgin, UT, USA

I thank you, thank you, thank you for being brave enough to share these messages…for going "out on a limb"…for having faith strong enough to "stand in the light" and to not shrink back, so that others may find their way Home. And for simply Being – and Being Love! Carol Twardoch, Atlanta, GA, USA

I am deeply grateful to Yael for having an ear for the most subtle and gentle voice from within her own heart, that started the flow of the living Messages from God to Humanity. God's ever present guidance found in her a devoted and pure voice with which to speak in the world again. With the Messages, God offers us His/Her hand to help us grow in Love and light and realize the vastness of our own true Being. He asks us to put our hand in His in trust, to surrender our little will to His bigger vision, so he can teach us about our own divinity. I am forever grateful to the Team of the Circle of Light for their deeply committed work and for all the Love that they are pouring constantly - like a well of living water, bubbling from joy – on everybody who contacts them. Metka Lebar, Ljubljana, Slovenia

Reading the Messages from God is like communing with God. Even if they are addressed to all humanity, they can also be a very personal experience. When you read the Messages from God, your heart will open and stay open if you so choose — a cascade of sparkling, fresh, flowing, colored Love energy. In Love from Love to Love creating more Love. I will be thankful forever. Tiziana Paggiolu, Sardinia, Italy

Words are so inadequate to describe how these books have touched my life… It's what I always thought relationships can be, and I never found it put into black and white. Here it was, so perfectly described. I devoured it like I would the finest "crème brule," not stopping until I had every last morsel of it, and then craved for more. It came at a time when I had said to my friends, "I found my Twin Flame," never knowing what it meant. Now I know. Carol Davis, Cat Spring, Texas, USA

DEDICATION

*To the Rings – those beautiful beings
whose hearts hear the call and
respond. Thank you, my
beloved Spirit Family.*

*To the precious hearts of humanity –
may our every breath serve the
awakening of your Love.*

Say "Yes" to Love,
Giving Birth to a World of Love

THE MESSAGES FROM GOD
Through Yael and Doug Powell

TABLE OF CONTENTS

INTRODUCTION

How can I tell you what it means to be the instrument through which these Messages have come? I am "the pen in God's hand," but I am also the feet upon the path. From the moment these Messages began in earnest — when my husband, Doug, and I came together – until now, every day I have been tenderly loved and patiently grown. Through the most personal, amazing and gentle Love, God has taken us from being two people filled with fear and pain, afraid of Love, to a glorious experience of joy together in which every day is a miracle.

Out of all that I have learned, all the glistening moments of transcendence, the experiences of awakening and of daily transformation, the greatest of all is the knowledge and experience of God's Love. It is so personal. It is sweet, tender, and completely unconditional. It is an experience of being bathed in reassurance, yet being lifted each moment into a grand perspective of every detail of life. God answers every question! This has been a continual amazement to me. And this glorious yet personal, vast but intimately present relationship with God is there for each of us. Its acceptance is the key to it all.

God has taken my heart and opened it with the utmost patience. With each step God became more personal, not less. How can I describe it? It is an expansion into the great magnificence, the glory of Creation, the ecstasy of ever touching more of the wholeness that is God. Yet with each and every expansion of my heart, God's tender Love was ever more connected with my life, and more and more a part of my experience of each moment.

How God can be the great Creator, so vast our minds can't gasp it, and at the same time be so intimately present, so personal and so tender is our greatest gift. It is a mystery to our minds, but as you read these Messages, your heart will know its truth—the truth that each of us is loved perfectly and personally by God. This is why I've used this word "personal" from the moment this experience began in 1986. No other word could describe this sweet communion or explain the seeming mystery of this great Love.

When I asked God how this could be — that we could have a personal relationship with the great whole of Love of which we are a part, God said to me that this is the wonder and the gift of our hearts. In our heart is where we meet God. It is the vehicle of our ability to relate to our Creator – intimately and forever. Our consciousness, God showed me, is that which experiences the oneness. Our consciousness is our energy that permeates All That Is and gives us the awareness that we are One with the All. Together heart and consciousness are the dance of life – the expression of our connection with God in both our intimacy and our vastness. God calls our hearts a miracle – a miracle for God as well as for us.

At first I was resistant to sharing these Messages because my experience of this communion was so personal that every nuance of my life was exposed as God led me beyond the world of ego. My ego, ever tricky, also said I was not worthy. "How could anyone be clear enough to be the instrument to receive Messages from God," it said, "let alone you"!

Then in the spring of 2000 I had a near-death experience. I went through what God called the "living bardo." I confronted every fear I'd ever had, and I discovered that I still withheld a little piece of my heart from God. I found I'd kept a little wedge between us. I saw that I still blamed God for my son's death, and that I still harbored shreds of doubt since "God had not been there for me," through all the pain and incest of my childhood. At last I fully gave my heart. I gave my life. I gave my Will to God completely. I closed that little gap where I held my little Will. Immediately I knew that I would live.

At that moment everything changed. What had been a "journey" of daily steps assisted each day through God's Message became a living transformation. My heart cracked open and Love became my life, and the Messages and experiences that are in these books began. These books are an arc, a trajectory, that has completely changed everything I thought I knew about life, about this world and about that which we call Christ consciousness.

Beginning with the book, God's Guidance to LightWorkers and going on through books beyond this one, these Messages create a bridge that God is building across which all of humanity will travel. It is a bridge of consciousness that takes us from our life in the world to our life in God. As we cross this bridge, we move from a world of duality – of light and dark, pleasure and pain, good and evil – to a world of unity in which there is only Love.

As these Messages were given, we at Circle of Light have been crossing this bridge ourselves, walking every step, asking every question, making every shift. Some of the Messages were answers to our questions. Others were streams of Love rushing through me outward to humanity. All were an experience of being lifted in such tenderness, such personal and uplifting Love that each Message has been a life-changing experience.

This Love will enfold you, too, as you read, for beneath the words and concepts are packages of Love being carried right to you to verify the content of these Messages and to bring you, too, into an ever-deeper personal relationship with God. God, the wonder-filled magnificence, while beyond our mental comprehension, is completely accessible through our hearts. You will discover, as we have, that it is within our very hearts that this bridge is being constructed.

Sitting in meditation nine years ago, God first revealed to me what I termed the "New World." It came about after a long conversation with a member of Greenpeace. She had carefully shown us proof after proof that this world was well beyond the hope of saving. The pollution was too high. The population was multiplying until soon the very numbers will prove impossible for the Earth to sustain. In deep distress after hearing this, I turned to God and asked if this was true. Were we here on a dying planet? Was it too late?

In answer I was lifted into a different view, another experience – that of an Earth of joy and gloriously rich abundance. I felt the peace. I shared a world of pristine hues and beauty in which there was communion between every form of life. Then, God clearly said: "There is a New World. But, you can't get there from here." Now I have more fully experienced this New World. It is not a place. It is a shift in consciousness. In God's presence, as I sit each day in meditation, the New World becomes ever clearer and the Old World fades away.

If your hands are on this book, you are ready, and nothing you believe about your life can keep you from traversing this bridge. Your heart now becomes your perception of the world, its reality affirmed as you read. You also are a bridge for all others who are drawn into your life. And so we build it, heart by heart, turning to God for understanding the steps, then giving the Love we are given. It is not too late for our precious Earth, nor will there be any "left behind." Instead, we are all in the midst of a miracle, part of which is recorded in these pages.

I "live my life" in a body filled with pain. I am often in bed, mostly "housebound," yet I spend my moments in bliss, surrounded by beauty, in ecstatic Love with my SoulMate. I share this simply as a way of telling you that no situation or circumstance can affect a waking heart or restrict you in any way from saying "Yes" to Love. As you do say "Yes" to Love and "yes" to God and rekindle your relationship with our Beloved Creator, everything that you have experienced in your life on Earth is "walked back" to Love. Then, because the Real language of the spirit is vibration or resonance, our lives connect by resonance to every human life that shares the same vibration of what we each went through. So we bring them back to God with us, closing the separation from God that's the reason for this world of duality. We bring humankind Home to Love with us!

God's covenant with us is that everything we believe with all our heart, God will help us create, for we are co-creators with God. Until now our heart's beliefs have been those of suffering and pain. These Messages from God are here to change this and to lead each one of us back to Love. This means Love on every level – the presence of our SoulMate beside us in this life, and the presence of our heart's belief in only Love, which will bring forth the world of which we dream. It is a world of such magnificence and beauty that each moment is a treasure beyond describing. That world is waiting for us, and these Messages from God are the bridge to get us there.

Yael
Circle of Light
October 2005

The Messages
From God

The moment that you realize
I Am available to you
and I Am personal
– in that moment
you are reconnected to
the truth,
your truth
as the deepest heart
of All I Am.
In that moment I begin
to lead you quickly Home
to the glory
that you are.

I Call You to a
Personal Relationship with Me

I Am calling each of you to a personal relationship with Me — so personal that I Am the living experience of your every moment. You are not only wrapped in My Love but we "see" each other — meaning that we know, love, and commune together, each moment of your life! Have I not explained to you that this is the entire purpose of this journey into ego? Was it not so that we could be close, so close, that you could be in Me but not lost in bliss? so that you could be in communion with Me as if we were One and yet we could relate?

I call you now to this personal relationship with Me that you may know the experience of divine Love as it flows through you — that you may also see that you are One with everything, yet ever you are yourself as well. As you realize this unity of All I Am as you as well, you will never again look on any part of Creation in the same way. Every human being shall be worthy of your total recognition — that whatever things they believed without Love, these things will disappear like mist in your Love.

You will never disregard human suffering but you will know with clarity the very truth — that they who suffer too have a personal relationship with Me. You can see Me in them, touching them, loving them, holding them in great tenderness. You then can relate to Me, in them, in a personal way. Can you feel this? Not only will you know them as yourself, resonating with the Love with which they are made. You will also see how I love them personally, from every angle. You will love them for Me. You will also be able to communicate with Me as I express within their life.

Some of you do not yet grasp what this will mean because we have just begun to open into our relationship, beloved ones. Even those whose lives are fully dedicated to Me have just begun to experience life as I will show it to you — miracle upon miracle of unfolding Love. Precious flame of life, opening as bird, dancing forth as flower, taking wing, growing deep – oh, all the beauty everywhere – it sings to you a special song, beloveds. It sings "in the key of ecstasy" and it is a conversation of Love to Love — to Love in growing awareness of itself.

I will reveal to you each life that you now meet through our personal relationship. You can see how ego in its quest for self-preservation takes even this and begins to alter it. Suddenly you find yourself off on some winding road of things you must do to finally be able to commune with God. Or you discover that, oh, so subtly, you've become involved in something else, without ever even knowing it! You've become involved in something that sounds so important – even opening the heart - but it has made us impersonal again.

This is where your attention should now be — all of you whose eyes rest upon these pages. *Our relationship is personal, a living communion of conscious Love.* Only knowing Me can you ever know yourself. Only the active participation in the living organism I Am can bring you into your fulfillment. There is only Love and it is ever given personally — one Love given and thus received, reflected endlessly in billions of glorious forms.

So whether it is loving your SoulMate or loving the Earth, loving a child or loving a world, every experience arises out of the personal *giving of Love.* Ideas will come and go. Techniques will always fail. But having – creating — the focus, the stillness, the freedom from the little mind and ego, will allow the Love to rise in you in an exaltation of movement as I Am personally in Love with you. To be alive is to be a part of the glorious action of the ongoing Moment of Creation — to be a part of an orgasmic bursting forth of life, a deep and gloriously vibrant contact, as will moves upon the deep of Love.

Thus even stillness of being is not enough. Yet out of stillness, ecstasy will rise every time, for the reverberation of the great moment, the LoveMaking, the movement is a personal experience for each of you – for every form of life. You are there. You are completely present in everything, every bit as much as I Am present in you. We are inseparable. Yet the very purpose of Creation, your creation, is relationship. It is so that I can give Love to you. It is so that I can know you and you Me and we are forever expanded in this miracle. A miracle it is that I Am and have such passion to give the Love I Am, and that you reflect that back to Me because you are strong enough to maintain your own identity right in the middle of the explosion of Love from which you are forever coming forth.

This, as yet, may be difficult for you to comprehend, but beyond Time you also are exploding forth. You are exploding forth from Me as I Am in the Moment of Creation, where I have become movement, Divine Masculine upon the All of the Divine Feminine. Because everything I Am is reflected throughout Creation, you come forth as exactly the same relationship – thus you are forever exploding forth in Love with your SoulMate.

It is a personal relationship we have. Beloved ones, this is the only answer, the goal, the focus of any and every spiritual path, whether you know it or not. It was originally the focus of every religion on Earth, as well – a place where people could gather to amplify for each other the experience of the ecstasy of life.

Think for a moment about the reverberations of the Moment of Creation! The All I Am in glorious explosion of life — the making of life by the movement of My Will to give the Love I Am upon the deep Love of My being. Think, beloveds, of the explosions of light, the dancing, pulsing, buzzing, singing exclamation of the creative moment. This energy is touching you now! It is bathing you. It is filling you. It is that of which you are made! A moment bathed in this life will shake you into ecstasy so huge that you are scattered like golden particles across the great pond of the universe!

Now think of current human life on Earth. Where is all that energy? Ah – now I reconfirm for you that every bit of your energy, beloved ones, is being taken up keeping out the ecstasy! Keeping it away! Pretending it doesn't exist! Oh, dearest ones, *if everyone released all the hidden effort this requires, the Earth would instantly become a living Sun.* This is not a metaphor. It is a fact.

Thus must you rejoin Me and allow Me to return to you your heritage of light. The moment that you realize I Am available to you and I Am personal, in that moment you release the lie. In that moment you are reconnected to the truth, your truth as the deepest heart of All I Am. In that moment, I begin to lead you quickly Home to the glory that you are.

Once I Am a conscious part of your life, nothing can stop us, beloveds. Nothing. You will wake into the truth of our Love. Even if takes you years to fully let it in it will happen, because of the power, the light, the ecstasy and the Love – the Love you are and the Love that reflects that back to you, your SoulMate.

Thus has all on Earth been going backward, reversed into a sucking vortex rather than a giving river, all so you could pretend for a while to be something other than Love. Into this, of course, have come all sorts of plans by little minds to use your light for purposes of fortifying anti-life, shielding you from all the Love you are. If you escape the little mind and touch the greater being, you are ready but not yet here in the explosion that we are. The greater being is the All of Love, the ocean of the Feminine, containing all Love and holding all within. But it still must have the Masculine, the action, the great and powerful movement "on the deep" for you to know yourselves. You must give forth, beloved ones.

Now I shall be personal, speaking right into your hearts, here in the world in which you live (not really). Perhaps it would be more appropriate to say the world to which you've led yourselves in a desire to experience yourselves with limitation.

Anyway, here you are, and one of you has asked the question: what of those with dedicated hearts but with no spiritual practice? What of those whose lives are found very much in the world? And what of my life personally? I shall answer every one. For some will find, when reading this, they will feel My living presence say to them, "This is your message." And for others it will clarify the confusing offers of enlightenment that pour upon the trusting minds of humanity right now. Do I need to sit and meditate? To chant and walk the labyrinth? To study this or that technique? To eat? To fast? To live on light?

Of course, you know the answer, but I remind you here as well. *Your only goal, beloved ones, is to have Me in your life, and you will have the only thing you need.* If I am here, recognized, then of course I will guide you in the perfect course of opening the petals of your golden lotus heart, of connecting every level and, most importantly, becoming that which you are meant to be. *I Am personal. I Am Love being given — given, beloveds, with the most passion, the most tenderness, the deepest care, the greatest respect for the glory that you are.* How I love you! Oh, how magnificent the moment when you turn and ask for Me. Not, "God help me" get this or that or something else. Not "God save me" from all the ego's machinations that tangle you up within your little self. But rather, "God, I love you," with an open heart, reaching out to Me.

From this comes the moment of connection. In this moment, all the heavens reverberate. "A child of God returns!" Thus do angels sing to angels. Thus do the Logoi sing to worlds. Thus do the stars sing forth in harmony. All Creation acknowledges the shedding of the fantasy that you are anything but divine Love in form. Thus do you prime the pump with gratitude, which helps release the hold of the gravity of ego. And thus do you begin the awakening to Love.

So here is how I answer each one of you. I have been calling you. *I have been calling you, specifically. There is work for you to do.* Although this is our natural relationship, this personal communion, humankind is spinning the wrong way. You spin around the worldly life instead of around Me, and this you must now change. I must be your focus. Me first. Me, Love, the center of your life. Me as I manifest in your SoulMate, yes, but in both cases, it must become a daily communion, a deeper experience.

It is not that your life in the world must change. It doesn't have to change at all. But your relationship to it must change. *You must be looking at Me when you look at the world — communing with me about decisions.* Yes, many of you do this! Not enough. It is time we are together, uniting in your consciousness each day.

Dear ones, I have said to you that as you come to completely know My Love for you, just so does your destiny approach. I ask this of you. Make the change in identity necessary to free yourself from the confines of this limited world. You all long for this, for the place where Time ceases and you are freed, freed from the physical and its meddlesome necessities. Here, of course, is the deeper truth of this. Time stops when you are living in relationship with Me. Time stops when your every moment is complete joy – even if you remain temporarily in the world. Time stops when your heart is filled to overflowing with Love, when you are lifted in the ecstasy of opportunity to serve our precious world.

There is effort required — the effort to overcome the gravity of the lie and those things that limit you that you have accepted as definitions of yourself. But just because some of you see the physical world clearly and work within it a certain way and others of you do this another way, on the level of spirit you are the same. Same vibration, same Love. However, you who are masculine are the active force while the feminine is the great pool.

Dear ones, you must exert the effort, put forth the energy to bring your consciousness more into alignment with Me. You must expend effort every day to lift beyond the pull of gravity to experience this communion. You must spend the energy and time needed to keep claiming this communion with Me. This is to be your spiritual practice. The focus is feeling My presence, knowing My touch, being available for Me to speak through clearly. What I ask is that each of you call forth this communion for yourself regularly.

Dear ones, it is time to give your life to Me. Do not be afraid that daily things won't get done, but rather, know that they will get done in timeless joy. Remember, this is about attention, about focus. It is not that you must quit anything. Simply replace your old-world thinking by coming into a new closeness with Me and a renewed commitment to accepting the deeply important part each of you plays in this work. Can you see how a shift in focus can re-orient everything? Can you see how this shift then defines where you apply your inner energy? How it makes the changes within yourself go deeper, to a new level of ecstasy, joy, life and, of course, Love? Then out of these inner changes the outer will spring, and Time and materiality will become less frozen and more filled with light.

So when others ask you, "What is necessary? What should our spiritual path be?" *You shall say to them – "develop a personal relationship with God. It is all that is needed to bring this forth for you."* Every path is different. For some it will be meditation. For others it may be simply shifting to acceptance. For others it may take great effort to come free of little mind. So again, each and every beloved person is exceptional and uniquely made. There can be no pat formula to success.

Yet once I am requested, once I am active in their life, their success is accomplished. The rest is simply peeling away the extraneous, the layers of illusion that keep My light from fully touching them. Your hearts are Mine. Though each path is individual, we know many things.

- ❤ Your open heart is the one and only opening through which we can communicate. Thus it will open as we come together, or its opening can bring forth our union.

- ❤ Your relationship with your SoulMate does reflect our relationship as well. Open to her or him, and it will bring you and Me closer.

- ❤ It will take some energy to break free of the backward swirl here on Earth but once released, all Creation's energy is available to you. (Thus once this is accomplished, your entire physicality will completely change forever into light.)

- ❤ Giving Love primes the pump and brings each person into alignment with his or her truth as cells within My heart.

- ❤ I Am Personal.

- ❤ Love Me until only I Am Real and you will have all of your answers.

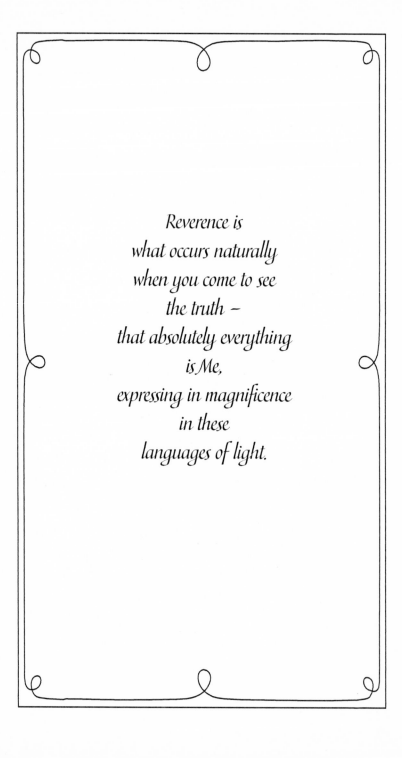

*Reverence is
what occurs naturally
when you come to see
the truth –
that absolutely everything
is Me,
expressing in magnificence
in these
languages of light.*

Reverence

All that I now give you will be beyond human language, for truly, we begin now to speak in the language of Love as it is recorded in light. Yet I will always also translate all that we do into words, so that the Book of Life is an open one, available for all to read. I am showing you the truth of pure experience, of Love as a living substance and the light that comes forth from it as it moves forth, always, to grow.

Creation does reveal itself to those who can see. It is to this reality I now direct you. I will show you how easily all of you can soar beyond all limitation, for the truth of Love always recognizes itself.

Oh, beloved ones, all of you, I have made you of the glittering, luminous, opulent and glorious substance of My Love. Now I tell you the simplicity of truth. Love always knows itself.

What is the key to this knowledge of Love's living truth? How do I share with you the glorious kaleidoscope of life becoming ever-greater life? How will you know that within the heart of a toad lies the DNA of light? That hidden within it is a perfect map of the glorious explosion of Love that is NOW? How will you ever really know yourself? And how are you to really know Me? How will you find the communion of Love, the unity of living light that is the New World? You are ready.

The answer is reverence. To live in reverence for every expression of life is to make the switch and to live permanently in the truth. To live in reverence will move you perfectly, and permanently, beyond the ego. Yet only when you are ready will it show you the way. Reverence is the "mouse button" that will switch the screen of your life. Yet, beloveds, it is so much more!

Reverence is ecstasy. It is the truth of Love, acknowledging itself. Reverence is the truth of Creation. It is how I love the Creation I Am, bursting forth within Me. Reverence is what occurs naturally when you come to see the truth — that absolutely everything is Me, expressing in magnificence, in these languages of light. *It is knowing that everything you see is a miracle of Love, for within it, whatever it is, I Am.* The truth of Creation is made manifest to those who can see.

Everything is alive in Me. Everything, then, is fashioned from My being. Even those things that are the sub-creations of humanity – they are still made from Love. They would have to be, since Love is All I Am. So even if you are "in the theater," watching the movie of illusion, you can see that the theater is Me. The film is Me. The very particles of life that can be shaped into a story are made from That I Am. The glorious creative spark with which the stories have a life at all – it is Me.

Every beautiful human being, every glorious expression of Nature, every animal and element, oh, all alive in Me! This same life is in everything. Once you come to recognize it, to honor it, to look for it unceasingly, you will have no barriers to experiencing it. In other words, beloved ones, now at this very moment when you accept reverence as My commission to you, all of Creation opens itself for you to see. You are no longer limited to Earth or your intellect, but rather have become a "seer" with the heart. Everything you look into, in reverence, will become for you an explosion of color, of dancing light, of living joy.

You will know as experience all that I have given you. All that you believed was theory, or tools, explanations, inspiration, will truly become for you our shared experience, for you are in Me. You are My living heart. Oh, can you now see that you can experience as I experience? You can love as I love? All that I Am is yours, including the ecstasy and the reverence for the magnificent life exploding forth as My expanding Love. Thus do you become the River of Life, experiencing everything as Love's unfolding.

Even the dream, even the illusion will part to reveal its truth to you — that only Love is living here! Only Love is growing. Everything else is "props" in the play of humanity learning they are Love. Yes, from this perspective it can seem filled with negativity. You must remember that Time does not exist. *All those lifetimes of pain and suffering are simply one of you thinking through a question about the nature of yourself.*

Thus must you now truly grasp the non-issue here of darkness, of pain, suffering, and violence. Beloved ones,

I now take you through to the truth. The illusion on Earth doesn't really exist. Using the analogy of humanity dreaming beneath the apple tree in the Garden of Eden is the closest your little minds can get. Yet when you walk through this doorway you will really understand that only Love lives in My heart.

Thus will you truly live as Jesus did – looking right through the illusion to the truth of Love before you. You will be washed in Love so passionate, so big and so powerful that truly your knees will bend before it. In front of you, as your brother or your sister human being, you will see the glory of Creation. Right there. And before your true sight will be revealed to you the glorious spark of their individuality as I create them. Not "created," dear ones. Create. Before you will be the magnificent unfolding of a child of God, the DNA of living Love, exploding forth before your eyes into a perfection of unity that right now, truly, even in your heart, you do not yet comprehend. Yet you will. You can. The key to it is reverence.

I am within each and every part of Creation. Thus, when you see this, when you become the "seer of the heart," you connect with the Christ in everyone. You connect with Love incarnate. So doing, that very light rises up to take you up to Me through them. This is very powerful, for it is ever the nature of Love incarnate, once freed, to leap up within the cell of My heart and to connect with the All I Am — beyond the incarnated self or light of Love. So does your recognition of Me in anything leap up to connect you to the greater Love I Am. In other words, the Christ is raised up to the Father – or whatever words apply to create the symbol of this union. The spark of

40

Love within is ignited by recognition and leaps into a glorious flame, higher and higher, until it leaps across the divide and is rejoined with the living fire of life I Am as All.

Do you grasp the significance? *Your recognition of Christ or the flame of Love within creates the connection in everything you see. Not only in you! This recognition is the healing of duality, the healing of anything that is not Love.*

You do not do this from "this side," dear ones, meaning from the little mind within the dream of separation. You do it only as Love, in the reverence that is God meeting God — God as Christ — embodied Love meeting God as the great vast explosion of Love That I Am.

In everything you revere, the truth of Love reveals itself. This I promise you. Yet words cannot describe the majesty of this. Looking into a human heart you will see it all. You will see the perfect pattern that it is, expressed as the luminous colors of living light bursting forth within them continually. As you allow your reverence to deepen, to be the greatest honoring of that which that person is, those very "codes of light" will shoot forth from within them as rays of light, joined perfectly in the most beautiful pattern with those who share the closest Love with them.

Then out beyond, and beyond and beyond, the magnificent pattern of Love will unfold, connecting, connecting, until you see before you the pattern of their created life. Then (oh, again, reach beyond words!) as the Love within them ignites by your flame and rises up to join the Love "without" (outside of the embodied spark), every one of the other connections are illuminated by the blaze. Thus as this person expands, awakes, is lifted up vibrationally, so too are all those whose lives touch his/hers (on the level of their truth as living Love).

Yet it is even more than this! Every single part of Creation is a glorious spark of My Love bursting forth. So every form of life will open itself before you as you gaze on it with reverence. You will look within to the truth of Love and like a glorious flower opening, each and every created life will connect you back to Me. In so doing, each will reveal to you the magnificence of the spark of perfect Love it is—and its connections to soul family, be they butterflies or barracudas! Dear ones, also revealed will be the connection of their kind to the larger glorious pattern of life.

Thus will reverence always place you on the frequency of highest truth. *If you live in reverence, you live beyond the ego.* Yet even so, ego is honored, not despised. It is loved as a part of Creation, a tool, a piece of life, of dancing energy that came to transcend itself. Just as My beloved Jesus showed, in raising up the Christ, the Love within, to Me, the ego is transformed.

Everything is honored, yet only truth revered. Oh, reverence is your natural attitude, for is it not magnificent beyond your current comprehension that I, the All, pour forth in Love into life multitudinous? Life. Expressed in numbers far, far beyond counting, in forms yet inconceivable – yet every life will take you perfectly to Me. Everywhere you look I Am. Consciousness is limitless, and Love, the life in everything.

Everything here on the Earth can and will take you directly to its truth as Love. You are developing the language, and the capability. All of humankind will learn that you can know the truth of Love in anything. As an example, let's use the whales. If you look into a whale, using your heart to see with, that very whale will blossom for you. Right before your reverent gaze, bursting into a kaleidoscope of breathtaking beauty you will know "whale." Knowing whale, you will know and honor every connection of whale to the greater Web of Life. You will know its purpose here with you. You will know its heart. Beloveds, you will know its immortality. For everything I Am, Is. Is, dear ones, as Love growing in the acknowledgment of itself. Becoming more Love – not ever less. Not ever less – for I will not ever be less than I Am.

Certainly you can see this. I Am God, the great All in whom lives Creation. Thus, dear ones, it is only a thought (a passing one!) in your co-creative consciousness that briefly entertains the impossible – that evil could exist, that I could ever be diminished in any way. It cannot happen. Thus, dear ones, you, humanity, in the next instant (in Reality) will come to the conclusion that it cannot happen! *One thought, dear ones, that is what this entire human/Earth creation (or sub-creation) is. It is you, the collective consciousness of humanity, the consciousness of the cells of My heart, musing together.*

This is seemingly "advanced thinking" here in this Earth experience. Yet quickly all will follow. You are like the first neurons firing in the brain when a thought begins to form. The rest of the neurons will fire soon, as the thought is fully formulated. You, knowing, begin the thought. You spark the whole process. Then you wait (and assist) as the other nerves catch up with you.

Such a magnificent and complex glory is Creation— the exploding forth of My passionate Love into every expression that I now imagine. Every one is born of union – the Two as One. The Divine Masculine (again words that do not capture the magnitude) of Divine Will and the Divine Feminine, the ocean of Love I Am, upon which Will moves to create. So in you. So in all of life. Whether yet manifest in the dream, All That Is contains these two elements. Just as you collectively grasp that Love is All, so too will this quickly become evident.

I am showing you, dear ones. I am now showing you the way. Through reverence.

Just as a seed
does hold within it
the pattern of its perfection
as the glorious fruit-bearing tree,
just so is such a pattern
within each of you –
the pattern of your perfection
in Me.

Reverence Now Becomes Your Way of Life

Reverence now becomes your way of life, for reverence is the timeless acknowledgment of the truth of Love as it stands before you. Each moment that you see reverently, truly with the heart – in that moment do you step beyond the veil. In that moment you are beyond Time, for you are in truth, not illusion. In that moment when you stop and shift and open into the heart's vision, in that moment you choose to see the Real. You choose to see life as it really is, not as you imagine it to be. In such moments you will truly be connected to every other spark of life that dances through Creation.

In reverence you approach life as sacred — as it is. You switch to the values of the heart of Love you are. You can live in reverence right in the middle of the illusory world, because in reverence, you are seeing every life exactly as it really is. Thus will you live in the truth, surrounded by the magnificence of Creation anywhere. In a city. In the country. In a nightclub. In the mall. Looking with reverence places you beyond the veil. It spreads around you the star-lit skies of eternity. It washes the world with light. Even in the thickest fog of illusion, you will see the truth.

How long all of you have mouthed the words that are your destiny: "The truth shall set you free." It will, dear ones. It will. The moment you move beyond the lie of separation, you see the unity of life. You see the precious center that beats within each human breast — not only as a speculation, but as your absolute and unshakable truth. It does not matter what piece of the "play" you see before you. It is irrelevant. When you look on life with reverence – the reverence that shakes your very being, that floods you with awe, that pours you out to wrap around life like a blanket – it matters not at all what form life takes before you. It is all Me. You now know the deepest truth of your being – that we are one. In this way will you grasp within yourself the magnificence of each person's truth as Love. In this way will you serve Love completely, asking nothing "for yourself," because we are one and we are Love.

You still remain in your incarnated life, but unlimited and free. This is the glorious gift of Christ! This limitless Love is within the embodiment as well as without. It is this consciousness, this being who holds My Love, My heart as form, that gives you the ability to know the vast Creation while clothed in form and matter.

You may not yet be able to grasp the magnificence of all embodiment. Suffice it to say that embodiment of all energies allows the focus of consciousness by which other life in embodiment may know, as experience, the truth of that part of life. Once you grasp this connecting light, when you shift your attention beyond the illusion, through these communions of Christ you may experience all Creation while you are in form.

It is difficult to speak of this in your language. The closest analogy would be telephone lines which allow you, even when not physically present, to deeply communicate and experience communion and Love with another human being. The fact of embodying consciousness is what allows you to know Nature Spirits, Devas, the Mother Earth herself, and soon the very heart of God as you come to know yourself.

But rather than rely on words for this, I ask you to experience it. Live in reverence and fully commit to the resulting experience. To do so you must shift beyond Time in order to look into each form of life and feel the experience that your reverence reveals. It takes only a moment when perceived with your heart. But it does take that moment. It takes the full connection with your truth as Love embodied, acknowledging the truth of that form of life as Love embodied, whatever life you look upon.

Reverence is a way of life, brought forward to you as the doorway through the veil by your Love for Me. It comes forth from the purity of your heart — by the "yes!" that your being says to Love. Your desire pours forth like sonic waves from you, pushing open the doors of perception and calling all who embody Creation. As you move across the veil, you will have the ability to experience any part of the glorious community of Love that I Am. Truly, that which you call the angels are My song of Love and exaltation in communion with My heart!

Dear ones, the heart's perception is limitless. It sees in all directions. Not only up, not only the vast magnificence of the All That Is outside of you. It sees the

All within as well. It looks not only skyward and outward, but inward just as easily. Both the world within your embodiment and the world within the Earth as well are visible to you. With greatest reverence, you now see your body with this same reverence — and the communities within the world that is your embodiment as well. For *you, humanity, are the embodying consciousness for the Earth*. So, you live and move and have your being within the Christ who looks within with reverence to touch your tender hearts and to honor you as part of Me. So, too, when you understand the truth of your vastness, will you tenderly and with greatest reverence acknowledge the communities of Love that you hold within your consciousness.

Let us return to the topic of your bodies. Oh, beloved ones, you are the embodying consciousness for this universe of Love! How humanity ignores this fact, seeing only through the eyes of ego the outer package of this universe. You have starved and maligned and abused, disregarded and even hated that which is yours to love. And yes, this is only a moment in eternity, but you cannot come to live beyond this "moment" until you embrace the truth. You must grasp that the heart's perception is beyond 360 degrees, for it goes within to other dimensions, through to parallel realities, and it perceives beyond Time. Thus are joined past and present lives, or segments of this imagining.

How will it be to approach your body with this great reverence? To look at it in the very way you might look upon the natural world? To see the light raining down into it? And to look at the millions of lights within? To see the same magnificent patterns within, as every cell and every atom unfold for you the pattern of life? And to feel the same total awe for the incredible beauty of absolutely every aspect of all that you, in consciousness, hold in form in Love.

You cannot love one part of Creation and not the other and step beyond the separation. Either All I Am is Love or it is not. So you will not live in reverence and Holy Communion with the All I Am that seems to be outside of you while ignoring the rest. I speak to all humanity. There are many ways that you each view your body, but so few live in reverence that, essentially, it is only those already ascended who choose to serve still as human forms. It is seeing yourselves as little bodies, separate from each other, looking outward toward each other and upward toward Me that keeps you believing in separation.

Once you live in reverence of every part of life, your vision is spherical, endless in every possible direction – beyond Time and every limitation.

Your bodies are congealed light, Love moving too slowly to be multi-dimensional. You have grasped that your beliefs affect these bodies and so you believe you can "make them better." Yet, still seeing with the little mind, you simply make them better containers, more to the liking of the standards of mass consciousness. Oh, beloved ones, it is time to ask: "what is my body, and how do I honor it?"

Can you imagine the Christ of God, the embodying consciousness of My heart? Can you imagine

51

Him/Her looking within (for of course, Christ is Twin Flames as well), and honoring in deepest awe and reverence every single human being? Revering you in the Real and seeing each and every one of you blossoming in majesty in the luminous colors of your unique creation? Seeing this with ecstatic joy in the glory of All I Am, that any of you meeting that gaze comes into instant recognition of yourself?

So, too, are you to the beloved community of living Love within you! Yet only with this same reverence will you ever come to fill your role and come into the incredible experience of being totally alive — of having every cell awake as Love, having seen as a community the truth of your gaze upon them – of having every atom alive as Love, thus revealed to you in your timeless reverence each and every one's magnificent and glorious individual uniqueness.

As above, so below. On every level. As Love explodes forth in the eternal Now Moment of Creation, it is manifested everywhere. Certainly within Me there are not some areas where Love is exploding forth and others where it isn't. This means that this same explosion of Love is manifest in All That Is — in every single quark, every increment of light, as Love moves forth to know itself in ever expanded ways.

Being My heart you have responsibility, dear ones. You have the responsibility to reverently be Love. And to be Love, all that you are must be recognized as Love itself.

So you must extend reverence to the glory within the cells of My heart as well as the great vast cosmos of Love's expansion. It is not enough to "fill your body with light." It is not enough to see your body as "perfect" in the ego's definition. When you are an awakened being, an awakened cell in My heart, you will grasp that your body IS Creation itself. *Your body will be millions of living universes that you have come to love.*

As you take responsibility (yes, that useful definition — response/ability) then the law of embodiment will mean that every atom within you is fueled by your heart and your SoulMate Love. Suddenly you will experience Love as limitless, as your very atoms come to dance in union with your Twin Flame, through the other universes embodied here on Earth. You will experience the Love you are, dancing through the embodied Love of other human beings and the embodiment of animals and elements and all of Nature.

Then as you awake into the real life beyond this thought of separation, nothing will be separate. Dear ones, this is the ascension. You cannot leave a part behind, believing it is separate, and be a unified being. The ascension, as you know, carries the body with it. So obviously (right?) seeing your body as somehow different, less than, physical, heavy, limited, and so on would not result in lifting the body into unity.

Thus do you become ever more available for the truth of Love to penetrate your consciousness. Until now, as you know, there has been a spiritual "autonomic system" by which your existence as life, as consciously directed

Love, has been kept going. Just as in your body, this system keeps you alive without the need for your attention, so, too, with humanity. It is the spirit that keeps you alive in Love with your "heart beating" while you "nap beneath the apple tree," dreaming that you are limited.

Once you wake the communities of life within you, through reverence and great Love, only then can you possibly know what is possible for you. On the downward or inward journey into form for these communities, it worked (and still does for some) to see the body as a dense "vehicle" to be driven by the spirit, or the soul, or I Am Presence. Yet now I take you further, because now the laws of life become evident to you. You can see that *only as you know it as unity can your body and your cosmos within expand into the unity of Love.* To hold it in your embodying consciousness as only a limited vehicle would keep it ever anchored there.

Thus does the Christ incarnate. You are now ready to gaze back into the consciousness of Love's greatest embodiment (My heart) and know yourself as that. As Christ. As Love in form. And thus knowing, you are ready to then lift this form, by your knowing, into that — into the totality of My heart, its truth — its truth as Love so vast that through it is all Creation nourished.

Look into your body in reverence, not "at" it. "At" is definitely the little mind seeing the body as different from itself. While you all grasp that your concepts can hurt or heal, you will now know that you, the conscious part of you, can and must see the body as consciousness as well as living light. *See your body as moving Love.*

Knowing this will provide you with ever expanding avenues of proof.

As you move beyond the definitions, even of Christ consciousness, you will find that opening filled with truth at ever-richer levels. As yet, you are experiencing the all of Love that is your reality through the limitations of the little mind. Only through reverence will you approach life from the correct perspective — deepest awe and gratitude for the endless possibilities of Love

You are not this body. This is true (this is continually proclaimed by very many people). You are its guiding consciousness! You are its Christ, embodying the consciousness of Love that is the cells of My heart. Thus, in this, once again is the whole repeated in all the parts. Just as humanity itself came forth into incarnation, separation, only to be ready to move upward, back to Me, so, too, do each of you come forth into your body in order to bring it back upward, back to Christ, the embodying consciousness of human life.

When you look into the mirror, look only with greatest reverence. Do so and the glorious community of living light you are will be a hologram, like Me (in Me). Within, you will see the flowering of consciousness of unity in every cell and atom. Instead of a predictable shape that you identify with, you will see the orgasm of Love. You will know the "fireworks" of your being in union with your SoulMate. Beloved ones, you will experience it all. That is when the Christ within rises up to join the All I Am. It is when the search is over and your identity is sure. It is when your living Love sustains you as you dance with Love throughout the stars. *When the vastness within you becomes joined with the vastness without and the body responds to the recognition, it is lifted up in Love.*

Do not worry about specifics, with words or definitions. Just keep embracing reverence and quickly you will be it, rather than thinking it.

Your body is more than your temple. It is your "warp drive" through which you will wrap your energy signature around the glorious universes and travel easily into the all of Love.

I Am with you, showing you beyond words the truth of your consciousness and your reality as Love. Believe only this and you will have your freedom.

*Even the most
magnificent vision of us
that you can possibly embrace
is only a tiny portion
of the grand and glorious Love
that we are.*

The Instant Truth of God— Being in Communion All the Time

Even here, on this one world, there are trillions of concepts of reality, and beyond this world there are trillions upon trillions more – oh far, far beyond your comprehension. Yet all exist in Me. Woven through every single concept, through every moment of experience, I Am. Through every interpretation, I am present. I am present in truth and I am seen and experienced always. Yes, always. The truth of My Love and its illumination is the energy of life itself, the substance of Creation, of All That Is.

So even in those who believe they have turned away from Me, I exist, and I Am known. I Am known by the very cells of a body and by the very spark of consciousness. I Am woven into the fabric of every co-creation and holding, of course, the true self of such beings.

Thus Am I the one and only common denominator in all life. So must you know that not only Am I with you every moment, but I Am fully present in all you see. Were I not, there would be no one there. There would be nothing to see, no spark of life to fuel even those believing they are separate from Me.

Dear ones, I Am to be your language. As you speak My name, God, then My presence within all things acknowledges itself. No, it does not matter what word you use, as long as the beings before you understand what it means. I Am the Creator, the life of all, in all, through all, the substance of which all is made.

If (when) you can see life as it expresses on the millions of other worlds — let alone all other dimensions and non-physical creations — you will truly grasp this awareness — that I Am life, and life is limitless. Yet every single part of life has within it recognition of the truth of Love I Am, the spark of life from which is manifested absolutely everything.

It is now time for you, dear ones, to accept at last the gift of our communion, of your ability to know My presence in and through your life. It is time now for our communion to be an ever-greater fullness, with no breaks in your perception. Only thus can I reach tenderly through you to spark to life the recognition of this truth in every human being. Only thus can you be purely Love in service to recognition of itself. I can promise you (and this you know intellectually, at least) that *every single human being is Me, exploring a new possibility of Myself.* And yes, sometimes they are pretending to be other than Love, which is why I must remind them who they are.

It is time for the "little you" to step aside. It is time for you to be, to live only in Me, only for Me, My heart and light. In every moment. You can each do this. Just as soon as you let go of the belief in duality, the belief that there is a "daily world" and a "spiritual life." It is now time for your full acceptance. It will come, for it is who you are. It is decreed by our agreement and by the great Love you have for Me. The moment you fully accept it, you will know a new level of the truth of life "on Earth."

You will know, beloveds, in experience, the world of Love. Now you are so close. Closer than your very breath, closer than a loving breeze that brushes you with gentle finger. Close.

Keep leaping into My loving arms. Leap into acceptance of the truth of life. Yes, in this moment. Ultimately, it is true for absolutely everyone. Yet I can tell you that belief is not enough. It must be experienced. It is only when you have no ego in you, only this experience of Me, that every person will see Me in them also.

In this leap will come the joy of life, for every cell, every atom, will then recognize itself. There will be no false barriers between us — only our communion. When you feel My presence expand within your being, you will allow it to overflow, placing whatever symbols are needed upon it to carry it forth to those I reach through your beloved form, this incarnation of our Love. I have explained to you that I must come to them through those who live here, grounding the living Love in the physicality of Earth.

Everywhere around humanity is My Love woven into the human creation to manifest the universal truth.

Thus is the Earth and Nature the expression of this Love. Though influenced by the human "mis-creation," the beauty will not be erased. It is held in place carefully through My tender living Love, cascading through the higher selves of humankind. Just as in your bodies, so in the world. Though it is a manifestation of your desire and Mine for physical expression, it also has its own intelligence, its own packaging of light. Thus will it continue to be the direct link to the real beauty of Creation, always.

As you shift into your higher vision, I ask you to look for these very streams of light running through every human life. They are often ignored, but always there. They are lifelines to the truth of Love. As we together touch My truth within each beloved person, these will become visible again, and we will guide humanity back into a communion with Nature that all might take advantage of this way through the illusion.

I ask you now to focus on our truth. You are only My Love in form. Every other identity and every other thought must wash away in the current of this living Love in motion pouring through you. You, too, must choose to experience Love only.

There is a very important distinction here. Many of you have been opening your heart and choosing to experience light, attempting to choose the perspective of your spiritual vision. Yet, dear ones, there is no "spiritual" without Me. I am the spiritual. Ultimately every human being will realize that true spiritual experience is a personal relationship with Me.

I am fully present in absolutely every part of all Creation. All Creation is Me growing in Love. You are all tenderly loved, personally grown, grown beyond any concept you can fathom. As you expand into the truth of our living joyful Love, you have access to everything else. I am what you call holographic. Every creation is simply a spark of moving Love within Me.

Thus, when you are ready — as you are ready — all you need to do is ask and I will show you anything. Once you allow our full communion, you can easily move beyond the confines of interpreting into language. You will then be able to experience all energies, all light — all that is the result of My moving Love, My being expanding in joyous exploration of all of Love's possibilities. It is glorious beyond glory, magnificent. It is a spectrum of moving light refracting into colors, which are a form within themselves.

You must only and ever see Love as limitless. You will also know that it is ever and always a personal experience of each and every being with the conscious Love they live within.

It makes no sense to separate the spiritual journey from Me who is the spiritual. The living spark of life you are is forever within Me. Nor does it make sense now for human beings to believe they must "climb the ladder" of spiritual progression. All beings available to assist are completely dedicated to connecting you to our conscious relationship. To see a hierarchy of beings is to then place yourself upon a long path of upward travel, a belief that is very limiting. It is certainly better than no spiritual goals or desire. Yet it too ultimately will have to be released. This is why our communion is the message I am pouring forth.

Only loving communion with Me is truth for humankind. All else here is your exploration of beliefs in separation, which are instantly and completely released by your reunion with Me. And rather than beliefs of so many different (and arduous) paths to Me, it is far more direct to come through the doorway of SoulMate Love, for in it you are accepting our truth.

Yet there is one thing, beloved ones, of which I must remind you. Do not limit Love. Do not form a set of assumptions or beliefs about the possibilities of either our communion or your Love with your SoulMate. If you do, then by these you will limit your experience until you are able to release them.

You are only and ever fully alive and available to the experience of the Love that you are in Me — awakening to the truth and the experience that you are My heart. *You, My beloved humanity, are the embodiment of My heart. You are the consciousness, as the oneness of humanity, of the vehicle of Love for all Creation. This, dear ones, is what the Christ is.*

It is the conscious enfolding by all of you together of the vehicle for Love and the delivery of Love to all that lives in Me — All That Is. Ponder this deeply within your own heart. Ultimately you must embrace this truth. Those who are what we call "Christed" are fully conscious of this. Christed beings are conscious of their complete union with all of humanity, and of holding within this collective consciousness this glorious heart of the All, the very heart of God.

A part of your true and vast being is still and ever present in conscious awareness of Love's delivery now. Were you not, none of this could exist! Yet to grow My heart, you are exploring us throughout a manifested universe. You, with your SoulMate, are the cell of My heart expanding the awareness of what Love can bring forth. Doing this strengthens your awareness of your uniqueness, which you will not ever lose. Thus is My heart expanded.

In truth, you are exploring yourselves throughout all Creation. As you grow into our full communion, you will re-open to these experiences. Certainly you must at least partially realize that My heart is vast, the vehicle of Love for All That Is. Certainly a cell of My heart would not be this limited as it explored itself.

You are, together with your Twin Flame, beams of magnificent creative light. Many beams of your living Love we have sent forth, each of which has created anchors on every level of vibration, dropping further rays of light from each. Now as you come back on the In-breath, as you draw up all of these beams, every new facet of being you have developed from your experience adds new color and new definition to the dancing particles of the consciousness of Love. You have increased this consciousness with every single moment of experience, increased it forever. And, beloved ones, just as your experience does for you, My experience of My heart, as you, will add to Me greatly.

Do not believe that this will be our only going-forth, either. For isn't one in-breath in your body followed by an out-breath?

I continue to stretch you. You can now see how easy it is to take this little leap before you and how imperative. In the face of all this magnificence, how can you possibly remain committed to the spirit-suffocating beliefs of humanity on Planet Earth? You are ready to embrace the truth of your limitlessness and your eternal forever relationship/communion with Me. What little invented belief system can possibly stand in the face of this truth? And this truth is now verified for you as you recognize the truth of the vast nature of your being.

That limited human consciousness could even conceive of a world without Love is truly unthinkable from the perspective of the truth. This is why Earth is such a fascination throughout all Creation! You have no idea of the attention now trained on you. You can, as a whole, hardly comprehend what you call UFO's. How could you all comprehend that there are consciousnesses, in whom this world is but a "blink," who still cannot resist the spectacle being played out here on Earth? And who, of course, pour forth, by the very nature of their consciousness, this very same communion with Me that I am speaking of with you. Thus, by their very attention, do they spark recognition within each of you of My presence in our life. So you see that the awakening here will be exponential. It cannot help but occur.

So, the great beams of light and moving Love that you are — you must now know that this always means together with your SoulMate or Twin Flame — have come forth into level after level, in every dimension and every vibrational scale of this "sub-creation." Sub-creation is a good word and would be useful to adopt. This is what I have been explaining to you as your higher self and as your enfoldment of the universes within this physical body.

I must tell you that your little mind cannot comprehend this. Do NOT allow yourselves to get trapped trying to understand this from that level. Do you know how many human beings are off in their own little bubbles of illusion, going round and round and round, pondering the meaning of life? Or pondering the way to God, or any other of the engrossing pastimes of the little mind? All of these can only be "sprung from the trap" by coming directly to Me, out through the side of the bubble rather than going around (and perhaps assuming they are making progress) within it.

All of this, dear ones, is given as perspective. So you can see that what looks to you like such a big thing is such a little leap! I implant in your consciousness the vast nature of your being and the grand design of experience. You, too, whose consciousness holds universes within it, are focused here to assist – as are the other vast "crowds" of beings focused here. You can now grasp how I Am the answer, for I Am the truth of Love. Once you let go of beliefs that are limiting (which ultimately all beliefs are), you can leap fully into our communion and in Me experience everything.

To summarize:

♥ Your experience of unlimited expression will be a
fact of your being and thus will convey itself to
others.

♥ You will have perspective (changing this is no
big deal).

♥ You will be beyond (way beyond!) any
attachment at all to how things unfold. You will
know as a fact that unfold they will, and that at
every level of experience (into forever) all that
you "know" must give way for the new to be
available to you.

♥ Even here in the jungle of density (jungle is a
very good analogy – better than you realize, for
compared to the vast open beauty of free-flowing
Love, this world is a jungle indeed), you will
know that you "can't get there from here." Only
through the leap into communion with Me,
beyond the little mind, can you get there.

♥ "Getting there" is as instant as you will allow
it to be.

♥ Important: even though you are functioning
in this seeming limitation, with body and story
to support, you will never see yourself as such,
nor will you see others as such! You will be
looking God to God — God in you to God in
them. I will be free then to reach through you

and claim My own, and you will have such conviction of this truth of their being that your very presence will "clear the veil for them" so they can see.

Dear ones, all you have to do now is let go. Let go of the little mind and all its limitations. For a little while, if it seeks to capture your attention, you will need to will yourself to Me. Oh, beloved ones, I cannot ever convince your little mind to believe in Me, to believe in us without doubt or fear. Yet just as I love you free, so too can you love it free. The life energy that is caught up in it and in the ego's all-out campaign to keep this dream in place, can be freed to be lifted and purified in your truth.

In Me you can experience All I Am, all the Love I Am unfolding, exploring and creating, growing. You can thus know that we are limitless. Then, knowing this, feeling it, it will manifest around you as life on Earth.

I have given you our focus — turning every single human being to the experience of Love, watching then as others so experience. Jesus was ever and always pointing people to Me, and though he has been misinterpreted, he did lay the foundation.

Now, having grasped the truth of Love, are you ready? Are you ready to let Me love through you? I send forth this wakeup call through every pathway. I will be knocking at the door to every consciousness. If the door stays locked, then eventually the Love within, in recognition of My call, will find a way to open it, which can be very disconcerting. Time is speeding up. What before could take a leisurely course of adjustment over years will happen fast and forcefully.

The door is the limited consciousness, the ego holding on. Yet even this, dear ones, even these descriptions of how we will love and how we will serve to awaken My beloved ones, these are Me working within you to open the door. In truth, when this door is fully open and you are living in communion and ecstasy, there will be nothing in you that relates to "saving" anything or anyone because you will be alive only in the truth of our limitlessness. This is another seeming contradiction, but only then will I really be able to love them through you completely. It will be very much like meditation. You will be with Me, yet you'll be aware of this body and experience as well.

Don't worry about making the leap. Instead, just keep making it in intention, thought and feeling, and trust that it will manifest more quickly than you think! Remember – it happens instantly and easily.

...every single human being
is Me,
exploring a new possibility
of Myself.
And yes, sometimes they are
pretending to be other than Love,
which is why I must remind them
who they are.

Change the Screen –
Program 1 and Program 2

Beloved ones, it is all right here — here woven in you, around you, inter-penetrating everything. I speak of the truth of life — the indescribable joy; the glorious, boundless freedom; the vast golden being of light that you are. And Me. Right here. In you, with you — dancing as the ecstasy of living light right through you.

Everything that you believe is you – it's Me. Everything you believe is solid – it's light. All the ways that fear defines reality are held in place by tiny threads so flimsy that in any moment of truth's recognition, they are severed. The lie moves away truly as easily as mist dissolves in the morning sun, because only belief holds it in place.

So far you have still seen all of this as "out there," "up there," or somewhere beyond yourself. The shift we are making is to bring it here — to understand that *truth and illusion co-exist in the very same space, and that all that is required is your shift in consciousness, and one or the other is in view.*

To give you an analogy based in your current life, it is exactly like your computer screen when two programs are open at once. The one you click on comes forward, temporarily covering the other. Yet the moment you click on the one behind, IT becomes the one that you are using. This analogy is perfect. I have told you that "The Fall" is happening now. It happens every moment you make the choice to run that program. Now. And Now. And Now. And with billions of humans running this program, it has captured the collective consciousness.

But that is all. *The moment that you "switch screens," you change the "program" by which you run your life. The moment that you "click on" truth, in the very same spot you are standing now, there exists a glorious being of light in limitless joy and ecstasy.*

Yet, dear ones, you must know that the other program exists in order to choose it. If that second screen is completely hidden behind the first, then somehow you must learn that there is something worth looking for behind the current window. You must also learn that you can "drag" the current screen away enough to see the screen behind it, in order to click on it and bring it into view. This is all of our training, the spiritual growth process, the part that seems to require time. But once this process has brought you here, to the point where you know two screens exist, then you can change screens easily, almost instantly, merely by deciding to do so.

This, then, is where we stand. It is easy. And (listen!) any moment you do it (change the screen), you have done it. Period. Not part way, not "learning to" or "growing into it." Just as on the computer, dear ones, you are either in one screen or the other. There is no in-between. This is what I want you to realize. This is the foundation of the shift. True, you can drag the front screen halfway, so you can see the screen behind it (to entice you!), but until you choose it, you are still working in the first program. Yet the moment you finally click on the other screen, you are fully there, running that program.

This is the perfect analogy, for what I want you to realize is that there is nowhere you have to "go." You do not need to have enough "light quotient." You do not need to lift yourself "up above" anything. All you have to do is choose the truth. Click the other program, and you are here.

In that moment, you reverse "The Fall." You say "no" to the serpent, for in that choice of truth you are moving beyond duality. There is no good and evil. Yet every moment a human being believes this — that there is a struggle, a battle, the potential for loss, lack, death and destruction — then there is. And billions of people making this choice create a very "solid" picture of reality for them.

The New World is won in every single moment that a human being "clicks the other screen." It may be only for a minute, but in that minute that human switched realities. Switched, dear ones. Even if they return to the old program, that moment creates momentum. It breaks the spell of the mass hypnosis. It says, in essence, that humankind now recognizes the truth. And moment by moment, the hold of duality is broken. Let Me repeat this for you. Moment by moment, choice by choice, the hold of duality is broken!

So whether it is seen as overcoming Maya, or returning to the Garden, by this process "The Fall" is reversed. Dear ones, because Time does not really exist, it is all happening NOW! Happening just as the dawn streaks over the mountains. That quickly. It is only to you, when you are in the old program that it can seem to be a slow process.

Is this not exciting? Do you realize just how many people now realize there is another program hidden behind the first? Well, if you do not, it will very quickly become obvious. As Time speeds up, cause and effect will be closer and closer and closer together, until it becomes indisputable to humanity that you create your reality, and you will get to watch as the sun of awakening comes over the mountains of illusion.

So there can be no "struggling with the ego." No lifting it up or overcoming it. All those tools were absolutely necessary to get you here. Now it is only choice. If you are struggling to lift up, you are in Screen 1, Old World program. Period. If you are in Love, in joy, in ecstasy, you are in Screen 2, New World. And just like the computer, the two programs exist in the same place, same space, and same moment.

In one, you are in The Garden biting into the apple and, because of it, judging yourself. You are feeling as if you are "naked," that something is wrong with you. Recognize this? And then, of course, by projection, you are believing there is something wrong with everyone and everything. So ultimately (on this bridge where you stand) you must realize that even spiritual progress is still

Screen 1 because it is believing you still aren't "right."

Screen 2 is Perfect Bliss. It is your complete union with Me. It is the awareness that we cannot be separate. It is knowing it's an impossibility! The Love you are as a manifested or incarnated being is the very same Love you are as a glorious spirit of light. This is why you have heard about beings who "ascended" in one moment, looking at the dawn or sitting in a field. The moment that you completely switch screens, then "ascension" is a possibility. Not a requirement. There are many beings on Earth who are here to serve while living only in Program 2, truth. Some are hundreds of years in their bodies. They don't need to ascend. They already "live" there! They are, like you, living as incarnations of Love in order to show the others that there is another choice to make.

So, dear ones, you are opening to the greater truth. We are one. One. Right here. Wherever you are. The heart is not separate from the chest in which it beats! And you are not separate from Me, and this process we are in, this awareness is the ascension of the Christ within into union with the Father That Is All. When the union is complete, the Christ within is the shining heart within Me. It is still the embodiment and the vessel of My Love, yet never separate – never has been and never will be - from My "chest," My being — the All Within which you serve in the delivery of Love.

In truth it is even beyond this. But I use these words to give all of you the sense of it. Later you will realize that not only are you the heart within Me that pumps forth the Love, you are the Love itself. You will realize that just as your heart is within you and you are My heart also, so, too, are you one with Me and *it is your consciousness that burns within as the heart of living Love.* In between all of these are you and I in everything — in every world and every creature, in every star-going nova streaming as Love, bursting in ecstasy, pumping forth life and nourishing it.

Yet in this moment you are here, focused in this little bitty teeny weenie (as you say) microscopic piece of our glorious explosion of Creation. In one moment, dear ones, you can shift the screen, and when you do, everything we are is available to you. The more you know this, the more of it you will experience. Growth on any and every level is ever and only this – you, all of you, opening your consciousness. If it seems like progression — that is the result of the pace at which you can open. If it seems instant, as in the ascensions we spoke of, that is how fast consciousness could open.

The purpose of those such as Jesus for humanity is to encourage your consciousness to embrace a larger piece of truth.

So even when you switch your program, how much of the truth of you that you experience is going to be determined by the expansiveness, or lack thereof, of your consciousness. Yet, even here, this is perfect, for just so are there those who can serve in the opening of the consciousness of others (or who choose to do so – knowing to turn back and give). Thus does it seem like there is a hierarchy of beings. Well, in a Creation this vast, there are going to be beings in all degrees of opening to the great and limitless Love I Am. That is part of the joy of it, even for Me – that I get to love all of you and in doing so to discover ever greater possibilities within. For each and every consciousness sees the All of Me uniquely, adds its special piece of Love to the pool of Love I Am and creates new facets of the diamonds within, refracting the light of My Love in new patterns and new colors.

I ask you to remember that all is available to everyone in the span of a decision to switch the program. You must always remember to look only to our oneness, to see your possibilities and to discover the expanse of your own consciousness. This is why I ask each of you to always bring others to communion directly with Me. For if you choose to keep your eyes on anyone else, you automatically adopt their perspective, at least temporarily. While they may be glorious when compared to human consciousness, and certainly they may be ready to assist you, dear ones, any one of you could sail beyond them as you remember who you are. This does not, in any way, belittle those who serve the Earth. It means only that each of you is unique. I ask you to wait upon My Will because you can't see "big enough." So must your eye be single unto Me, for I am truly limitless. Coming to Me, even now, here in the Old World, sets your consciousness on limitless rather than on progression.

Thus is the shift truly into your spiritual consciousness, but not the spiritual consciousness as viewed from here (although this can be a step in the training). Instead it is shifting screens. Suspending this program. Choosing another. Returning "the apple," moment after moment, until the truth becomes your only screen — until you close the program named "Old World." Knowing who you are, you then take within you the others' hearts, into the truth of Love we are. Just as you did for your own ego, so you do for theirs. Help them switch the program. Just as you did with your heart, you will do with theirs.

You will take their heart within our vastness and recognize its light as beating in our chest, for so it is, of course. The consciousness of the person doesn't know it, for he or she is still exploring the moment of choice. That is all this is. It is you, dear ones, all of you, having gone forth to solidify your unique identity as cells within My heart. It is you, collectively, together, entertaining the question: "What if I believed there is other than God, other than only perfect Love?" All the rest of this is exactly as often happens with you. You ponder a question and then suddenly you are lost in your own mind, picturing possibilities. This is what is happening. So, to continue the analogy, you are all standing in the Garden of Eden (your perfection as Love), lost in your fantasy of possible answers to that question.

Every life of every soul is a different one of these scenarios, answering the question, "What if there were other than the Love that I am?" All of the progressions of souls learning their lessons is your greater self reminding you as you wander through our dream. So seemingly the universe is full of learning souls, incarnating and incarnating over eons of time. Yet in truth, you are still standing in the Garden, being co-creators, living out all the possibilities.

Yet, beloveds, just as for you here when you sleep and you do at last awaken, you will have the very same experience. (It is true – "as above so below" — since your dream is you, dreaming). The dream that seemed to go on forever was in truth only the moments before waking. The alarm clock is ringing. Time to get up from your nap. How long will it take you? Will you keep incorporating the wakeup call into the dream? Will you hit the snooze alarm? Did you really believe there was other than good? This is the fascination. Thus do others crowd around, monitoring your process and offering assistance. Sending in telepathic messages, "This life is but a dream." They even go into dream time with you to bring you signs.

So though we switched analogies, you get the picture, beloved ones. Those who wake, yet choose to stay, are especially applauded — not in an ego sense but in recognition that even here the truth of Love can exist. Giving. Being alive in Me while yet reaching into the dream time to bring to consciousness those still re-creating the belief in good and evil and the belief in separation right in the middle of complete unity. What magnificent quality has made you choose to sojourn here? To stay lost within this fantasy? And what amazing strengths of consciousness will you bring into My heart upon your waking?

So you will not remain in ego. You will switch to truth, and you will trust that as you do this, every moment anchors it more firmly in the collective consciousness. You know that ecstasy is its hallmark and complete unity with All I Am is your Home (yet ever is your consciousness your own, though we are unified in/as Love). Out of choice will you walk among the dreamers and retain the ability to see their dream. But it will be as a fantasy, misty and unreal. You will see negativity only to remove it as you help them switch the screen. Yet you will still be able to speak the language of the world – but only to give them the training and reminders of the truth of Love they are.

As you embrace your truth as Love and live within our unity, so will you truly wrap each and every human being in the blanket of your Love and unfreeze them with your ecstasy together with your SoulMate.

Do not accept the little mind as part of who you are. Instead, keep choosing to switch to Program 2 – your truth as Love. You will wrap every human being in your Love, see them only as Love, and speak the Old World language only to bring forth the messages of truth into their dream or fantasy. Thus will you/We truly be delivering Love as We, as living light, infuse their being while they sleep beneath the apple tree in the Garden of their truth. You, however, will be entering their dream for but a moment, delivering, as we said, all of Our Love directly to their being while their ego barely notices, or keeps talking to itself.

You will see how it will be/is, when you are in ecstasy, in Me, in Love with your SoulMate, and you are in the world for others. You will open your mouth and We will be speaking. Love will pour forth from you to them and you will feel only ecstasy and Love, life and joy, exuberance and the absolute assurance of perfection as yourself. You will by choice be in this world, but truly not of it. The only divine emotions are Love and

joy and ecstasy and life! Life abundant. Life perfect.
Choose to have these. Choose to switch screens. And
know that every choice does accomplish it.

Do not come "up" the ladder anymore. That is
done. Come into truth. Merge with Me. Join in Love.
You all know this truth. Just keep choosing. Open your
heart and switch. Leap directly into the New. Directly
into Me. And if you happen to switch back, simply
choose again. It is easy. You will continue to serve within
the dream. But you are not to accept the little mind, the
ego, or the duality as yours. Rather than confront it or
ignore it, I call you all to choose again! To push away the
apple. Know that if you do so successfully, all of Program
1 will simply fade away for you. You will not have ego,
though when in the "country," you can use the language
if you must to get the message through. If it does not
fade, choose again. Choose until you are successful, until
you are in My presence, in ecstasy. And then simply,
when necessary, choose again.

The analogy I have given you of the computer will
be one of your most effective teaching tools. It will also
help you to grasp the difference between dreaming of
awakening (thus having to deal with ego and little mind)
and waking, which is simply coming directly through the
veil of the dream right into the ecstasy of your truth.

Ecstasy is your truth, dear ones. And life
abundant. If you do not have it, you are in Program 1,
fantasizing about Program 2, or dreaming you are waking.
This is still very much a part of humanity's process – the
tools, the quest, the "aha" experiences. But for each of

you reading this, it is now the choice. Easy, and it carries its own proof.

I am with you. Remember judgment, even of the "fact" you are "back here" in the ego is all illusion. Simply and joyfully choose again. And before you know it, you will be easily in ecstasy as Program 2 becomes more and more the only one you run.

When the acorn that contained
the individual pattern
is cracked open
and the oak tree grows,
the acorn becomes compost for
the continuation of life.
So is it with your ego.
When you reach the point
of desire for only Love,
then that which contained you
and held the seed
of your glorious perfection
is shed easily.

The Truth About Fear, Unveiled

Dear ones, I am bringing you through the doorway. I am joining each of your hearts with the consciousness of My greater heart. I am opening your hearts until the heart itself is that very doorway through which you shall step into our greater union — Love into greater Love — the individual will into the greater Will. Every sense, every thought, every breath, will be lived within the greater All of My unending good, My great and glorious blessing. I am naming as Mine everything you are — every particle of your great being and every hair upon your human head.

Yet each of you will need to meet Me. You will need to exert the effort to move yourself beyond the inertia of the human ego and into the greater spiritual life.

There are many such doorways, beloved ones, in the growth of My heart as it recognizes itself. Even that which is the greatest vision on the horizon of human consciousness – what you are calling the ascension – is only a tiny piece of it. How could it possibly be otherwise when I Am All There Is! Oh, precious heart within Me, how little you can fathom the great body of God within whose chest you beat. How tiny the fragment of your own consciousness you have yet uncovered!

So part of this experience will always be this reminder to humanity. Even the most glorious and magnificent vision of us that you can possibly embrace is only a tiny portion of the grand and glorious Love that we are. If it weren't, then I would not be God. I would not be worthy of the spirit that is alive within you.

You are sparks of a truth of Love so magnificent that it encompasses eternity. It embraces all Creation. There is nothing greater. Yet even I do not know the boundaries of Myself! Even I do not know the reaches of the very Love I Am. So no matter what you reach, there will always be more. Oh, it is the truth upon which life is created. It is also the bane of the human ego – that which likes to believe it can be the "best."

It is here that we will begin, for I tell you that to walk through the doorway of truth is the greatest possible experience of true humility. Once you are beyond this little dream, dear ones, you are breathing with eternity. You are beating with the great pulse of Love — vast beyond all imagined possibilities. In this great experience, even the human ego must "bow its head" in reverence.

So first you must now realize that truth will take care of the illusion. Love, as it washes through Creation bringing life and nourishment, will take care of the human ego. Once the truth is experienced, the ego disappears. This is the natural progression. Even Nature tells you this perfectly. When the acorn that contained the individual pattern is cracked open and the oak tree grows, the acorn becomes compost for the continuation of life. So is it with your ego. When you reach this point of desire for only Love, then that which contained you, which held the seed of your glorious perfection, is shed easily. Like the acorn, it becomes simply empty husks.

Just so, dear ones, do you approach this moment. Truly this is only a moment in your life as a cell of My heart, and so do you come forth to shed the shell, to become the oak tree in the forest of God. It is a good analogy, for just as a tree, do you continually give up each form of your development in service to the whole.

It is this that is the key in the lock upon this door. It is not "spiritual attainment," although that certainly plays a part. No, once again this is the distinction between pure and perfect Love and the deception of the ego. Spiritual attainment without the true giving to the whole of Love is only an ego play, a theater in which a human being plays to amuse himself/herself — plays, dear ones, to the audience of others and not to the truth I Am, and only has the ego as reward. Yet as you know, this can be what you call "tricky business" as the ego can be very eloquent and convincing. It is learning this distinction that is the real spiritual growth. It is the cracking open of the "acorn" of the precious human heart, which opens to reveal the passionate dedication to serve Love beyond all thought of self. Only through this will the door open.

Now, having said this, I return you to the topic of co-creation. You will now understand the true nature of this term. What many are currently focused on, named "manifestation" or "creating your reality," is only this game of ego. Yet this is the "higher" distinction for which many are not yet ready. You who are reading this will know the truth and will live the truth. You will set the pattern that when others are ready, you will be the cutting edge upon which they will crack open the acorns of their hearts.

Beloved ones, it truly is only when you have given yourself to the service of the greater that you are freed from ego. To you I say tenderly that it will happen naturally and easily when your one desire is only and ever to be the servant of divine Love. I cannot describe for you in words this difference, but you know it in your heart (and in the hearts of those around you). You know it when a human being comes to recognize self as nothing but the vessel through which I pour My Love.

Then you are ready, because – listen to this distinction – co-creation is the service to creation. Nothing less, of course! Your heart recognizes its truth. How could it possibly be otherwise? You are ready to create, to claim your heritage, when you, like Me, serve as the vehicle of Love for Creation.

Obvious, isn't it? Ah, but certainly not easy! It has taken billions of years in the accounting of Time to get you here. And also obvious, you cannot pretend. You cannot pretend to be here when you are not. The ego always shows itself eventually. As I have ever and always told you, all creation holds to the seed of its conception. So even if a person believes he or she is serving Love, they will know that they are still serving ego when they observe what appears in their life. It is infallible.

There are two causalities here. One is "like creates like." The other is spiritual service. Many such as you who read these words have come to walk the pattern – to walk the labyrinth of creation, that others will understand. These, however, know who they are (though the ego will often deny it). Yet regardless of which position you occupy, you will always feel that pattern. All human beings feel the pattern of Love that lives within them. I guarantee it. But the ego is a stubborn energy. It essentially throws up smokescreens "like crazy," as you say, to keep a person from recognizing this pattern.

So, dear ones, the ego will raise up every possible distraction. Some of these are valid and important pressure points. The ego will sometimes seek the "release" of energy that feeds it. Sexual orgasm without true Love consciousness, drugs, anger, daredevil risk-taking for the adrenaline rush, gambling are all examples. This mimics the true nature of growth in Love. Love does a similar thing, though at a more universal level, seeking to be given rather than seeking to get. However, Love does also build within the heart of My being (you), building up the energy needed to shoot forth in great waves to wash and nourish All I Am.

This pattern is experienced throughout Creation on every single level. On the grand level it is you, My heart, generating the energy needed to push forth the "blood" of Love that nourishes the All I Am. Within each cell this is you and your Twin Flame in glorious sacred sexual union, building up the energy of Love, electrically charged by that sparking of the + and – charges you are, until it explodes forth to fuel the pumping forth of Love.

Within you, this is your own heart, resonating all the way up and down the vibrational field of Creation, pumping forth Love!

It is first the all of My heart, the Christ. Then it is the cells, you as Twin Flames. Then it is you together, holding forth as universes of thought and Will expressing Love. Then it is the Logos here (oh, there is much more in between, but this gives you the idea), the Logos as Twin Flames of one being, pumping forth Love to humanity and Earth. Then it is the cells within your Twin Flame hearts (on the scale of My heart) that are these bodies, these human beings.

Then joined together here on this level as expressions of Twin Flames you already are, it is the two of you consciously pumping forth Love to unfreeze and bless humanity as you make Love as sacred sexual union. Then, dear ones, it is those cells in your hearts, each one of your bodies, also reflecting in every one your own vast Twin Flame energy, each one firing electrically to pump the blood of Love forth to all your body. And on and on it goes.

I have skipped many levels here of the "as above, so below" truth of Love, but you get the idea. In each and every one of these levels, there is a building up of energy and then an "orgasm," a release of energy powerful enough to push Love forth. Oh, in this do so many secrets lie. Study this, beloved ones. It will show you everything.

Now, back to ego. Now you can see that (a) you have a deep inner recognition of this process, your participation on every level with the great orgasmic Now Moment of Creation, which I have continually shown you; and (b) the ego can usurp this position. The ego creates enticing but empty situations that mimic this natural rhythm of the deepest knowledge of your entire being, substituting these empty shows mentioned before (addiction to any and every sort of situation that can bring a "rush" of energy that mimics the true orgasmic nature of Love).

Initially this was not a negative thing. Initially this was to help you stay connected to the rhythm of Love so that you would recognize it. But you know what happened. Humanity became so absorbed in this ego rush that you collectively forgot to look up. You forgot to look beyond it to the pattern it represented. Ultimately, as you see here on Earth, the mimicry became the goal and the initial purpose totally lost.

Fear is exactly and perfectly this. Let Me explain a little further. Consider this perspective to help you grasp this. Your normal pattern is the orgasmic explosion of Love. Think of yourselves as hearts with electrical nerves that fire to assist you to keep beating and pumping forth Love. Originally, Love would be essentially the activation of the neurotransmitters. When you looked at your SoulMate — at this level, even when you acknowledge Love — then that Love fits itself into the "receptor" of your being (your emotions) and "fires" the circuit of yourself, causing you to pump forth Love. This is your function as a cell of My heart. It is and always has been your only function. Love is given forth. My heart beats. Your heart beats. On every single level this is the natural course or rhythm.

At some point this part of you we call ego, determining not to crack open and be superceded, made a huge discovery. If the natural order was reversed, the resulting neurotransmitter still worked. Instead of pumping forth Love, it pumped forth fear. However, what happened was that Love was not given, so Love then was not received. Thus the ego was never superceded. What was meant to be an opening into more (more ecstasy, more joy, more discovery of ourselves) became a closed circuit, going round and round on itself.

It fulfilled your natural expectation. It feels like the natural order of things because it accomplishes the same building of energy and the release. Only the building is completely focused inward on the little ego self. Thus does your powerful co-creative attention keep creating this little self's self-serving contained circuit of getting, not giving. But there is a "rush" of energy after a buildup – the release of which is powered by adrenaline. It feels so "natural" that it becomes addictive. Fear then, as you know, has become the perfect tool of separation. This was never meant to be. Neither were all the offshoots of adrenaline rushes and addictions. Once the ego got the hang of it, using your own co-creative power turned upside down – well, you can see the result.

Now, back to the beginning of this. Once you recognize that this syndrome of fear and addiction mimics the natural order, you can make the shift. You can shift back to your natural state, the state of exploding glorious ecstatic Love that is the nature of all life. All, dear ones.

Even Me. As you live within My being, Love is your very truth forever. Exploding forth on wings of ecstasy (not adrenaline), Love nourishes every particle of Creation. Understanding the similarity between the usurper and the real, you can now switch.

So, now you understand My revelation that your own ego has been showing you this pattern perfectly – drumming up any and every possibility for fear. Now that you grasp the situation, at every juncture you can chose Love.

This is a major shift. It is the shift completely out of the illusion of fear and into the full experience of Love as all there is. Yes, there are levels where seeming evil exists. No doubt about it. Yet every single consciousness there uses fear as its means of communication. Thus once anyone is beyond fear, to that person evil ceases to exist. So do I hold all of you in tender comfort for the terrible experiences wrought by the perversion of the natural order. Yet simultaneously I show you that Love and fear cannot co-exist, for they use the very same "nerves" to access you, the same systems of energy. This information is very important in your role as way showers for humanity. With this whole explanation of fear and Love, you will be able to break the hold of fear over My beloved children! Please catch this vision.

I have given you the information on the shift from ego to the heart. Now as you move beyond the ego, I will be able to show it to you clearly. Then you will have information for setting free those you have come to serve. I tell you that all the beautiful inspiration and visions of truth I have given to you will amount to nothing if we do not assist our beloved humanity to break the addiction to fear.

This is why many of you have known fear so intimately. You must know it inside out. Yes, there is a great shift in energy now occurring. The veils of the illusion are thinning. But fear is a subtle and tricky addiction (for the ego is fueled by your own divine intelligence!). So it can seem that those awakening are turning easily to Love when in truth they are still backwards and focused on ego, sometimes experiencing the cheap thrill of fear and advancing the cause of separation, while mouthing the principles of unification.

Now please stop right here and realize that YOU do not (and never will) need to know which is which! You do not and will never need to determine who is caught and who is free. Beware the tricks of your own ego! You need only know the joyful experience of your own release and the tender sharing of this with others. I will bring the others home to Me. I need you to reach them where they live. This is why you are in bodies.

Now I ask you to return to our communion. Your heart is completely open, pressed up against the greatest Love ever known – Me, your own greater truth, the Creator I Am. And in humanity, you became the other question, the reverse polarity, "Can God I Am be anything but Love?"

The answer of course is No, and this remembrance is the entire truth of this coming time. It truly is the return of Christ in you. Christ is Love incarnate. Not fear. Only Love. Thus as you help Me release My own sweet cells from this little lie, humanity will embody the answer. The Christ is only Love.

I ask each of you to now embrace this Love in every way, to reclaim your spiritual sight. You are being readied to be only Love, conquering some of the "strongest" experiences the human ego can give. There are many who can see the shift and who believe they serve humanity when in truth they serve the little self. There is no judgment here. They too will awake. Yet *it is this intense training to see the truth and to really choose the heart that will serve as the lifebuoy, the rope to safety as the veil thins and Earth rises up.*

Exciting times! Yes. And critical ones. Thus do I ask you for effort. To take this seriously – the great oxymoron – to take seriously embracing joy! Yet it does require energy, dear ones, and determination, to make this shift — to reclaim your real sight, your true vision and your experience of complete trust in good.

Give everyone
that which you want yourself –
recognition as
the clear and perfect Twin Flame
Love they are.

Relating to Those We See
as in the Illusion

You are as yet very tender, all of you who would now hold forth the truth – tender shoots in the Garden of God, because while you are touching the New, being lifted into this pure light of truth, you are also still alive in the world of form. You are still subject to the encroachment of the illusion into your consciousness.

For this reason I ask you to walk very carefully – to proceed only in deepest prayer, to have your eyes only on Me, your hearts entwined with your SoulMate, and your will given over completely to Me. For it is this line you walk which is the thin rope bridge across the chasm between the old and the New. And, yes, I need you here, standing on the bridge, bringing the others to Me. But you must not look down and you must not look back. This, at times, may not be easy, for you are not yet perfected, not working as "Ascended Ones." Yet you are in a sense going to be filling that role, for I am pushing My humanity to you. I am invigorating the life within them that they can't help but want to grow. Yet you, beloveds, cannot identify with them. As just said, you are not quite free.

Thus you must realize that, first, the illusion can still hook you. Secondly, as I have said before, that very hook may be used for teaching – for nothing now happens in you for any other reason. Even so, *I must alert you of the necessity to be absolutely vigilant about your powerful attention.* You must learn to see only as the Masters do. Yet you are not completely free. How will you accomplish this? By giving your will completely to Me.

Beloved ones, to give your will is to give yourself, your all, your entirety, your wholeness. It is to give your hearts, yes, but it is also to completely give your consciousness. It is to give Me your mind as well as your heart and soul, and to let Me love through you. Oh, beloved ones, please, this is the only way that we can accomplish what we must do. It is your heart's desire, I know, for your hearts are truly Mine — to turn and reach for our beloved ones, all the precious hearts and souls of all My humanity.

Only if you allow Me to think, Me to speak, and Me to love in every single minute, will you be sure of success – and thus I Am sure through you.

If you allow Me to see through you, you will be on your knees, dear ones, loving each one. You will be holding them in your gaze as if they were tender, newborn chicks and you were the one they imprint upon. Oh, you would see how fresh they are, how vulnerable, and even how confused. What must the world look like to them – to all those who cannot yet see the truth?

Oh, beloved ones, this world is so confusing, for everywhere they look they see only mirrors! Somehow out of what they see flashing around and around again, they must try to make sense of life.

Thus must you allow Me to reach for them. Allow Me to love them perfectly, for even your definitions of their reality are impediments to the flow of Love. Precious ones, in any place where your attention is drawn by them, where you have opinion or you have resistance (and even the most subtle forms of judgment), these are places the illusion still holds you, which further impedes My flow.

Beloved ones, you cannot expect yourselves yet to be perfect. Yes, I ask you to aspire to this, but remember what I have told you before – that you cannot even imagine your good? Well, dearest ones, you whose hearts are so beautiful, so dedicated, of yourselves you cannot do this either. Of yourselves, you cannot be this bridge, cannot do this work. For these two worlds are still very different.

So I must love them through you. Only this can acknowledge you, for that is the way the Masters live. They are completely and fully alive in Me. In My Will, as My Will, and seeing only My perfection, they attained their ascension. So will you, beloved ones, but this cannot ever be your goal. Your goal can only ever be to give, for of course you know that is All There Is.

Thus do I now ask you, as the moving rivers of humanity begin to flow toward you, that your daily, moment-to-moment prayer is continually to be only My Will. Only My Will. Love only in the sweet peace of ecstasy and wait until I reveal to you the truth of every life before you. I now promise you that as you give yourselves to Me and wait, I will always show you the truth of the person I have brought to you. I will show you their truth in Me. I will show you how I love them. As My greatest gift, I will send forth through you the image of My truth in them.

What does this mean? It means that I will reveal their perfection. I will show to you, My beautiful servers, how it is I created them — what piece of My perfected heart they hold, once they remember who they are — just as I also hold forth for you, that you may see yourselves. I used the word "image" of their perfect selves because, as yet, it will still be a reflection of the glorious truth, but an ever-clearer one.

Then, beloveds, you will know. You will know what it is I am ever and always bringing through to them. You will then see exactly how you can assist by using what is now manifested before them in their lives.

Suddenly, it will all make sense. Yes, you will see where their ego has deceived them – how their ego skewed the truth to keep them from remembering. But you will also see just how I am working in their lives to bring them back to Me. Oh, you will see once again how I use every crack, every possibility. You will see how, if I present their truth and the ego distorts it, I will come right back to use the distortion itself to bring them another possibility, another clue in their search for themselves.

Certainly you see, each of you, how perfectly I have done this with you – how carefully I brought you here – how I use everything to teach you — how I repeat and repeat and gently and lovingly repeat the truth in any way that you can possibly understand. You remember how painstakingly careful I have been, inserting one tiny little expansion into the highest of our current thinking. How you can now go back and see how everything was there – every truth, waiting for you to be able to understand – and only now are you beginning to grasp the things I was giving then.

Oh, beloved ones, you can have no judgment! You can have none of the "prince of this world" as I send you into the midst of it. The only way to accomplish this is to give yourselves completely. Give yourselves to Me, to Love, to being ever and only the vehicle of My expression in this world.

Know that whenever you want someone to be other than they are, then you (the little you) are present. To your little minds this may not make sense, for surely I am always growing you. Therefore, your little mind or ego will think that I, too, must not be satisfied with where they are. Dear ones, here is the truth. *Just as a seed does hold within it the pattern of its perfection as the glorious fruit-bearing tree, just so is such a pattern within each of you — the pattern of your perfection in Me.* It is that which you are, and which nothing can take from you. When I see you, I see this truth. That is who you are to Me — the beautiful, oh, glorious magnificent all-encompassing perfectly unique expression of My Love!

As I see you, as I turn My loving attention upon you continually, what I see is this: I see the perfect you. I see it burning within you. Glowing. Shining up at Me. All I do is acknowledge it until you notice – and that moment of your noticing, of your acknowledgment of our truth as I created you, that is what changes your life. Can you see this? I do not ever see you as other than you are. The fact of this continual acknowledgement of your truth creates a magnetism, an upward pull. Continually. Always there. Always tugging at you. The moment you can let in any bit of it, at that moment the magnetism of truth pulls you through the illusion, upward, closer to Me. (We are speaking vibrationally here, of course.)

To you it seems that I am ever using every tiny opening – but in truth those awakenings, realizations and changes are the result of your upward glance. The moment you look up, you release the pull (or gravity) of the ego and My Love simply pulls you upward. In your life this looks like certain discoveries, learning experiences, and so forth.

As you allow Me to love through you, to see through you, to use every bit of your being as the vehicle for My magnetic Love, you will see people rise. You will see them recognize themselves through you. They will see themselves in your eyes. You will see their lives change. **BE CAREFUL — *for of yourselves, you do nothing.*** I don't even need to tell you of all the gurus and teachers whose ego found a way to come back in by convincing them that they were "special," and that they had "saved" these people.

Beloved ones, truly do look to Jesus as your teacher. What he successfully did was allow Me to use him perfectly. When he looked at anyone, he saw as Me and he knew it. He saw only the truth of each person. Those who acknowledged it, who turned their gaze to Me because of him, were healed. They were freed — because right then they released their ego, and My Love magnetized them right out of the illusion! Jesus knew that he did not "do the works." He never, for a moment, lost sight of this. He completely delighted at waiting for Me to show him My truth about everything, and any passages that may seem otherwise have been clothed by the judgments of those telling the stories.

So while he did lovingly allow Me to show, through him, the illusory nature of the attachment to money, it was those whose egos were very threatened that recorded it as Jesus having anger. I can tell you he had none, for he truly did wait on Me for everything. That is what it means to be Christed.

Speaking of such, of course as you live only to give, so will you ultimately receive. As My Love pours through you to others, it will lift you and lift you – until without ever putting one bit of attention on it, you will find you have ascended. For what is ascension but coming into your own full truth in Me? Gazing ever upward to Me, all gravity of the ego will disappear. You will simply and effortlessly rise into your perfection, and still serving Love, ever seeking to bless, to be the perfect vehicle of My Love, one day you will truly realize you are no longer "acting as if," but rather you ARE the Ascended Master.

How will you dialogue with those that you serve, with those still deep in the illusion? By saying these words, over and over in every possible way and then waiting for Me to show you the answer:

"How can I help you?" "How can I help you?"
"How can I help you?"

"How can I help you know you are safe, you are loved, you are worthy of joy?"

"How can I help you turn your eyes upward to God who is now, at this very moment, seeking to love you through me?"

They will answer you! And so will I! They will hold out for you perfectly where the illusion has caught them. I will hold out for you, perfectly, the truth of their being. If you, as the little you, are not in the way, you will see absolutely, exactly, how to show them in just the right way, with just the right words, who they are in Me.

Then you must leave the results in My hands. Beloved ones, you must also remember this. Truth has its own time. Each person has only a certain spiritual energy that they have gained with which to resist the pull of the illusory, the false world of ego. So you might have to wait for years for your opportunity in them, for you currently are here with them in Time. But what does it matter, if all you do is ever give your will to Me? Whether it is this moment or a hundred moments from now, it doesn't matter, since in every one you are ever and always allowing Me to love them.

As you love Me with all your heart, mind, soul and strength, that Love clears you, prepares you, connects you perfectly with Me, that I can then love through you. Can you see how (always!) perfect it is?

The more you love Me, the more I can love with you, through you! Thus, the Love you send upward to Me magnetizes My Love to you. It touches the pure light of moving Love. It calls forth the very highest vibration, and then by the law of attraction, it pulls it back to you. It connects you to the glorious sweetness of My living presence, pouring through you to all. So you are blessed also, for of course you continue to benefit from that which your Love for Me has become. You are blessed by the Love I can now pour to others through this gloriously open heart that you are.

As each of you is grown. then every blessing you receive also blesses your SoulMate — another great blessing from your humble willingness to serve Me. Thus will your relationship grow and be blessed in amazing ways as each of you contributes to the growing of both together. So does the masculine perfection complement the feminine perfection, and each of you becomes perfectly rounded out.

I can tell you forever of how Love grows you perfectly. Your inherent perfection brings you upward to Me the moment the gravity of ego is released. Dear ones, you can trust this in others also. As you serve, you simply need to ask Me to show you, to reach through you to demonstrate how to release the pull of ego through the vision of perfection, without ever going to the ego's level.

Ah – isn't it exciting, this glorious birth of Love? More people every day are seeing glimpses. Our work will be easy, dear ones, as long as you remember to allow Me to do the work.

Oh, beloved ones,
you are walking
this entire path of Love
in physicality,
and to the greatest purpose!
For while you swim
with all your might
upward
to the Light I Am,
so do you carry with you
the entire weight
of the consciousness
of humankind.

Releasing Our Identity
as a Limited Human Being

With every moment of the living Now, I Am a Love Song being sung to Myself. I Am the discovery of Love! What it is, how it feels and of course, what it does. Most of all, I Am Love, Real Love, forever and always celebrating the truth of itself.

Love is forever free. Nothing can contain or bind it. Nothing can ever stop its flow or dampen its explosion. For what Love does is give itself completely, unconditionally, being willing to give so much of itself that it becomes transcendent. Turning into a greater Love or more perfect inclusion, a total embrace so that in the fires of Love's alchemical nature, Love becomes more – more of itself, more of its nature. Love is a transcendent fire that only knows its true nature in the burning.

So when you love, you cannot hold back. Not even one tiny iota. All must be given with such passion and totality that the flames of transformation are lit from within. This is how we love. Yet though I use the word "we," because we have this dialogue, there is no "Me," no "you." There is truly only Love, growing in awareness of itself.

Thus, dear ones, you come now to another moment on the altar — another moment when Love asks of you to give yourself to it — to give yourself completely — with not only no reservation but with passionate acceptance of the explosion of your heart.

As you do this, My beloveds, you become transcendent. The heart of Love in the living Now takes you through the background/foreground shift. Then you know yourself as spirit, as the living heart of God, and you can feel that which is spirit, Love's magnificent consciousness. This dream life on the Earth truly becomes the background — the speck on the bottom of the screen.

Now feel how you love the beings who are alive in the world. There is nothing before you but God, nothing but the one Love we are. Where is the "speck" of their human life? It is barely discernable. It is one little pearl held in the "oyster" of their being. The moment each person wakes to the Real and the truth of her/his Love, the pearl itself also becomes transparent, transcendent life, for even the pearl is Love. Because nothing else exists! It is a dream and you are waking up and My heart is truly ecstatic. It sings in celebration! All the life I Am is available to you. But not only to you but as you, the giving heart of life.

Beloved ones, first we built the bridge and now you go across it. This is very important. For the bridge that we built is a bridge of awareness, the conscious comprehension of the truth of the Real – that there is only and forever Love, giving itself in ecstatic explosion and knowing itself by that which it gives, Now after Now.

***Come now across the bridge and leave behind
your identity as a limited human being! You are the
heart of God.*** Yet even this definition is so limited by the
mind, for heart implies a center point, yet mind can't
comprehend at all that the center IS the whole and vice
versa. You approach the glorious alchemy of the living
Twin Flame spirit, and you can ever and only do this
when you do not limit yourself at all. You can only live
and be this Love when you comprehend this oneness –
that everything you perceive is always a refraction of this
one light of living Love.

Beloved ones, you can do this work that you are
here "on Earth" to do only when no longer encumbered
by a false identity. The background, foreground shift
that I have been showing you for years is the releasing of
your false identity as a limited being and the acceptance
of the Real truth of your life!

Now, let Me show you where this is leading you
here, in your service. As you release your own identity as
limited human beings, you will no longer see anyone else
this way! For you are seeing and drawing in front of you
those of like resonance, yes, but it's even bigger than this.
As long as you see yourselves as human, you cannot see
the others before you as the pure heart of God. Thus, do
you unconsciously amplify in them the duality and the
person you see in front of you is not the truth of them!

All are the one heart of Love — not some who
have "done the work," nor others who are "starting to get
it." Outside of the pocket of reversal, the illusion,
everyone is free. So if that upon which you focus is that

which you amplify and if that which you give forth is also what you receive, then how you perceive each precious life is not only the reflection of you but also what you receive in terms of energy.

In this, beloved ones, if you can perceive it, is a pivot point upon which the shift can occur, for if you are truly at the center point, then there is only one thing happening – the heart of God, awake — fully and totally conscious. So in this "place" of the center, whatever you choose to perceive is reflected in every direction. You can, at the center, standing on this bridge, focus on opening your own Twin Flame heart. You can focus on awakening to your own consciousness, and you can focus on seeing this awakened heart consciousness before you as everyone that you shall ever encounter, and all are the same.

This is because there is only one thing happening – the "reversing of the reversal," the freeing of all life on Earth, the "taking back in" of all the projections of the decision to perceive separation. Now. There is only one. One life. One light. One sound. One Love, and the only way that you can do this is to leave all of the false perceptions behind of a life outside of Me, outside of Love.

So, beloved ones, I have said to you, "what you focus upon, you 'worship'." What you focus on, you create. Therefore, please open your hearts to now realize that you truly must *give everyone that which you want yourselves – recognition as the clear and perfect Twin Flame Love they are.*

The mind will convince you that humanity is best served by helping them see their ego. But your heart *knows the truth. Humanity is best served by helping them see their perfection*, thus being for them the opportunity to see beyond themselves!

I need each of you in our Oneness, present at the center point. No other point will do. Ah, but the shift now is to take your focus off of ego and the old false identities of old heart's beliefs and to place your focus on the shining light of this glorious Love. "If thine eye be single," beloved ones, again. Just as we have spoken of before, on some level each event is happening, but I ask you to keep your focus on the highest truth you can comprehend – the single "eye" of the living heart of the one Love I Am.

Talk to those who come before you by speaking of how the light makes the old heart's beliefs show up and that this is the work they must do, to shift their whole identity to this truth and wholeness of Love. Tell them the truth as you know it and let Me do any translating that's needed. Ask them to keep holding their heart to the light until, in the Love and the oneness, they are able to "go Vertical" and to be in the Real.

Remember the words, "what you focus on, you worship." And know, dearest ones, that I have so carefully guided you to this new awareness that is in the process of totally transforming your life – the background/ foreground shift — from an identity as a human being opening the heart and consciousness to the identity as the living ecstasy of your identity in the Real — the ecstatic Twin Flame heart at the Moment of Creation.

Hold those words, each one for a moment, and you will instantly feel this truth about focus. Remember that life in the Real is only perceived through the heart. While heart perception is natural, here it has been forgotten. Please choose this focus on heart perception and choose to stay out of the mind and its thoughts. Then there is nothing blocking the experiences of pure Love — the one Love we are.

Soon this Love
will be guiding you
through the pulses of
My heartbeat
as Creation pulses out and in.
Free from beliefs in
a limited life,
you can be
unfettered magnificent Love,
awakening all life on Earth
with your shining and
precious heart.

Which World Will You Choose?

Each day, each hour, each moment now, My call comes to each of you – the call of the truth of your magnificent heart. It is the call that asks you to choose.

Beloved ones, the time is here – the time you have each known since you came to Earth to serve. It is the time in which the waiting Love, ever present at the center, calls every human heart back Home — Home to its truth in the Now. Home to the acknowledgement of its place as the heart of Creation, when the pulsing light that is the Moment of Creation passes through the center of the living Twin Flame heart.

Which world will you serve? Where is your Love? Is it hidden within an identity of the ego-mind as a limited human being? Or is it pouring forth as the Love of My heart to the winging, singing song of the atoms of light?

Creation is a hologram. This you believe that you know. But now, beloved ones, it is time for you to be this, rather than to know it. At the magnificent Moment of Creation, the explosion of light that is the coming together of Divine Masculine and Divine Feminine, the Love I Am — once resting quiet — is suddenly bursting forth in giving. The movement of Love is the emission of light and that great star of exploding light at the center of the Twin Flame Love I Am is expressed everywhere within the whole. This expression is full and magnetic. It comes forth all at once. So the Moment of Creation shows up as dancing star fields of living Love, living Twin Flame hearts, living Twin Flame atoms.

At the center of every atom, then, is the Moment of Creation, exploding forth as a star of light, pulsing with the "heartbeat" of the one great Love I Am. So, beloved ones, if you turn within to the center of your Twin Flame heart, or to the center of an atom that is alive within your being, you are instantly present. Home in the Real — completely in contact with the ongoing Moment of Creation.

Touching this center, you have total access to the great hologram of Love we are. These are the "jump points" or the StarGates to all the dimensions of consciousness. Most of all, they are the access points to the very Now moment when you come forth, again, from Me.

One touch in consciousness with this living StarGate of the whole and you are fully immersed in your truth as Love, as the living giving Love I Am. One moment's touch of your heart with the center of your greater heart or the center of an atom, and you are totally immersed in the experience of your true being – that you are limitless and you are Love. You are Love's unending consciousness. You are My Love being given. You are the Love itself. You are the whole heart. You are each a living part of one of the two great streams of consciousness.

You are truly the living Twin Flame cell at the center or heart of Creation, given life each Now with a purpose, a tone, a resonance of the one voice that you may contribute to the Great Song. You are given life, blazing forth while receiving your identity, your unique resonance from Me — Now after living Now.

You are the Twin Flame presence, and you welcome life with reverence – accepting the light and nurturing it in your own Twin Flame Love as your atoms join, Making Love with your Twin Flame. On every level this moment is alive in you and given as My Love — alive in the River of living Light. These things you can feel as you return to your center, as you go within to "find out who you are" — the consciousness of Love, unlimited, ecstatic and totally free. This is the choice for the Real, the glorious Oneness.

In the outside world, as you know so well, there is physical life — some beautiful and some horrible. Every life seems limited in, oh, so many ways — limited by forces outside, by Nature, by others, by the weather, and limited by the feelings that create so many reactions. The most obvious limiter of those physical lives is death itself.

You know the outer choices well. You have made this choice so many times that I need not go into it, except to say that this is not the truth. Death is not a part of life, nor is it a part of Me, of us, of the living Love we are, the great and glorious Oneness. This brings Me back to the question again of which world you choose, which world you serve.

All of you know the meaning of "these times," the return of the world to Love. Yet the deepest truth is, as you also know, *you ARE the Love already*. What keeps you from deeply living this truth of Love is the false identities of ego.

Beloved ones, now I want you to feel the difference between these choices – the outer world with its chaos and strife, and the inner world of limitless Love, of magnificent dancing light, a "world" that is the All of Love, the whole of this Being we are. Feel this by going into the realms of consciousness, by your focus on that center point, that center of your heart.

You can go through the doorway anytime, at the center of your heart, to feel and be and experience your "beingness" as Love. You can release the world of the ego-mind for this time that you travel within. Or you can transform all the identities you have held as a limited human being. You can bring them right into that blazing center and let them be transforming in our meeting.

In this moment of exploding light that blazes every Now through your Twin Flame heart (and through the heart of every atom), this explosion is the moment where your Twin Flame life comes forth. It is the blaze that is the birth of life, the orgasmic Moment of Creation. In this light you now exist as a unique and limitless being. In other words, this blazing light is the moment of your creation where you take your identity from Me.

Anything you bring to this from the false world of the ego will be transformed instantly by the explosion of this Love at your "birth." It is worth everything. As you already know, there is nothing more important.

Only when you no longer see yourselves at all as a limited human being, only when you feel in your deepest heart that you are this eternal Love will you "love and move and have your being" in Me. Only as you live this Love and breathe this Love, only then will you be choosing to live as who you really are, a being of pure glorious Love. Only then will the world you choose be the world of Love that is the bridge world to the Real.

When you are this Love, then it reflects your heart in every dimension. You then become a "hologram" as well, with every part of your life reflecting the truth of your radiant heart – including your life in the world. Then, as you take each step in Now moment after Now moment, the expressions of Our one great Love are a resonant field around you. Everywhere you move your focus, Love is there, supporting you.

First, you'll feel the Love. Then, if you choose to participate, you'll see the symbols of that Love here, as the things in this world. For when you are alive in consciousness, you are dissolved into the whole, ever aware of your beloved Twin Flame, ever aware of My Love but neither one is separate from you – like notes within a song. You are present. Centered. In the Now, beyond the perceptions of Time.

Yet, as you use your heart's field to focus through, you can choose the one degree of separation that allows you and Me to have relationship and shows you your Twin Flame clearly. However, beware (or be aware) – more separation than this and you enter the "old world," the world of collective duality where you are lost in your ego-mind's identities.

The foreground of all life is spirit. It is the energies of living Love. The light of My call, My intention now brings this shift in focus here to life on Earth. Those who do not have connection to the heart are going to need you very much, dear ones, because they will have no reference points, no way to navigate the realms of consciousness. Therefore, you must choose right away, that the resonance of Love alive in your hearts can attune them to the patterns of the living Love we are.

Experience the living Now. I use this word, living, to make things clear to you – that this life in Love is not ever just a "void," but that rather, it is teeming with the countless joyous streams of life, each one unique, beautiful, deeply Love and deeply loved, alive, ecstatic, exuberant and filled with unending joy.

Do not believe the world of the senses, the world of "two eyes" anymore! For the change comes now on the inner and not from the outer at all. So many of you (My LightWorkers) keep looking at the outside world and waiting to see the changes in how life on Earth is happening. Yet, beloved ones, the outer world as you know it is now ending. So to look outside of Love, outside of yourselves for anything is fallacy. *Life comes forth from within.*

You will feel the change before you see it. You will feel the hearts of your brothers and sisters opening. You will feel this Love reclaiming you, reclaiming every life on Earth, for each life can take their identity only from Me.

Live through your hearts and silence your little minds. Let your hearts be open and receptive and I will live through you. Sometimes, if you have the one percent in place (using your heart to perceive Me), you will "receive" My Love and My guidance, dropped as instant awareness into your awaiting heart. If you are completely still and centered at the point of light, the radiant star, then ....

I will simply live you – in you and as your Love. Both of these are valid, especially here in service. But beloved ones, please be careful, be diligent, and train yourselves not to "fall off center" and into the ego mind. Then you perceive as outside of yourself all that comes forth from within – your life, your abundance, even your Love, your "needs" of every kind.

In truth, this world is only living light, atoms that are connected at the center to the Real, to the Moment of Creation, and most of all, to this Love. This Love is your life, your wealth and your nourishment. This Love is your true identity. You already know this. Yet it must be everything to you. *You cannot find the doorway unless it is the priority of your life.* I can promise you that, beloved ones, that nothing is more important.

I Am your Love, and I Am this Love in All. Right where you are at this moment, the doorway to the Real is everywhere, all around you, shining in reflection to your glorious Twin Flame heart. Yet though it is reflected all around you, it is entered from within. The reflections come from your own heart's center. When you know this, they can lead you there, back to the living Now within.

Soon this Love will be guiding you through the pulses of My heartbeat as Creation pulses out and in. Free from beliefs in a limited life, you can be unfettered magnificent Love, awakening all life on Earth with your shining and precious heart.

Which "you" will you choose, dearest one, this Now moment and the next? You will easily know if you're successful by what shows up, reflected around you.

I Am with you. I Am in you. I Am you. Thank you for accepting this transformation of your life — from limited human being, subject to the whims of an "outside world" to the very heart of Love I Am, full and perfect (and Making Love!) every single Now.

The birth of Christ within you,
beautiful ones,
so deeply blessed,
is the choice to remember
the truth of Love
as the only truth
of who you are.

Birthing the Christ
December 2004

My beloved precious humanity, each year at
Christmas I come to you more present and more
perceivable through the thinning of the veil. This is a time
that with the birth of the light at the Solstice, there is an
opening in the veil. Each year I come to the door of your
heart and I ask you, deep in the silence there, if you are
willing to birth the Christ this year. Are you willing to
acknowledge Love shining in the heavens of your being, a
Star of Bethlehem just for you, announcing the coming of
the Christ?

Christ is living Love. It is the essence of your purity
as a living glorious deeply alive, totally cherished forever
en-lightened part of My living heart. Christ is not about
religion, for it cannot be claimed by any man or woman as
resting specifically on any one life.

It is the truth of My Love in All. It is the living
reflection, here on Earth, of the magnificent Love of which
you are made — each of you and all of you. Alive in My
Love forever. Christ is the word that I use to describe the
heart of God that knows itself, not as a limited human
being, but as the All of Love in service here to the
remembrance of who you are. The birth of Christ within

you, beautiful ones so deeply blessed, is the choice to remember the truth of Love as the only truth of who you are.

For beloved ones, there is only Love. I promise you this. Everything else appearing here is a figment of your imagination. It is a dream, a belief that you can be separate from Love. Yet deep in your heart you know the truth. As I knock at the door of your heart I am asking you to make the choice for Love.

What you believe is everything, for as I have told you before, our covenant is that whatever you shall believe in your heart I will manifest. Believe in Me, I whisper now. Turn your precious attention to the light within your heart. Investigate the truth of Love and then compare it to the ego-mind and realize that what you focus upon IS what you choose.

Choose Love, dearest ones. Say "yes" to this light. Choose reverence for this glorious Love of which all things are made. As soon as you do, you will realize that we cannot be separate. All I Am is Love and Love is that of which you are ever made and in which you have your being. But, you have to make the choice to believe in Love first, before the truth of Love will be evident – for what you believe, we create.

Thus do I come now to wrap you in Love — to sing to your heart the song of your spirit. I lift you, awake now, from the dream that Love can hurt you, from the belief that we can be separate, and especially from the duality which is simply your belief that something else can exist other than the Love we are.

Right behind the illusion of a separate life and a world full of pain is the living pulsing, glorious truth that Love is All There Is. The living Now is forever new, the magnificent union of the Love that I Am and the will, arising Now after Now, to give of the Love that I Am. Right here, precious ones, is also you – forever a living expression of the Moment of Creation. You also are that which we name the one heart, made of the living forces of Creation. You are Twin Flames of Love, burning with each other, dancing together in passionate embrace, echoing in My heart the glory ever alive, ever Now, of the Moment of Creation. Yet, to be this Love, to experience it, you must first believe in the Christ in you – that Love is who you are.

The choice must come first – the choice for Love. Only then can this light of Christ alive in you become that which reveals your true Love — true Love as your identity, received from Me through your precious open heart. True Love as your Twin Flame, the one who is the living proof that you are Love, alive as Love in Me together, the living Double Helix forever.

Beloved ones, this light of Christ is already alive deep in your hearts. It has never wavered, never even flickered. It burns in glorious ecstasy both night and day forever. It is the longing for pure Love, the longing for reunion with Me that in the truth beyond words is the Reunion with Me.

Say "yes" to this light, beloved ones, please. Hold your focus here in your heart until it joins with the great Love I Am. Ego-mind then fades away in the power of your focus. Your heart becomes available for Love to live through, and because of this, Love becomes your life in the world as well.

There is much I could explain to you, but pure Love is very simple. Will you answer the knock when I come to your heart, each moment, this Christmas time? Will you choose to know "the Christ of God" deeply enough to know it as yourself? Will you allow the illusions of a life separate from Me and thus separate from Love to fall away? The moment that you do, the human falls away. The Love that is Real then becomes a living experience. It is anchored here on Earth through the presence of your heart.

You are the Bodhisattvas. You are here to see humanity as they really are – billions of expressions of My one great heart alive in Love in the ecstatic explosion that is the Moment of Creation – a moment that never ends.

Choose this Love. Let the torch of your heart reveal that you are Love in service, and that as you shift to your heart for perception, releasing the ego-mind, your heart will reveal in everyone the same magnificent flame, the two forces of life forever Making Love, and that Love is All of Creation.

Why call it the Christ, this living flame of Love that is your Twin Flame heart? Because it is the "embodiment" in consciousness of that which is My heart, the living heart of All. Yet, first must come the "yes," dearest ones — the choice for Love, the release of the dream of ego-mind that

Love can hurt. Only then will the flame of Love become the torch that shows the truth of Love every Now, forever.

This is not simply an uplifting Message. For all of your lives you've been searching for this Love. But you were searching through the ego-mind, looking outside yourself to find it when it can only be found through the doorway of your heart.

Open this door and your Twin Flame is here. Open this door and know you are the heart of God. Open this door and you will be free, dearest ones, of the dream of the little mind. You will be alive in the living Now which is the actual Moment of Creation.

The longing for Love is an inner experience, pulling you through the veil by the act of deep remembrance – of going within, leaving behind Time, returning to participation in the Moment of Creation.

Words can never capture this experience of the living light. But once you've chosen deeply and felt the truth beyond the dream, nothing on Earth can ever satisfy you again except becoming Love — joining in the living Now with your Twin Flame who is a part of you – just as you are a part of Me and yet forever known in relationship through the gift of the act of Creation itself.

Let Love become your only truth, your guiding light, your focus. Then beloved ones, the light of Christ will be your living heart, connected forever to that which is Real, the magnificent wholeness of Love we are together, not ever separate, yet aware of a precious relationship.

Creation is a gift. It is the moment when pure Love, the ocean, the stillness is moved upon by the lightning bolt of My deep desire to give My Love. In the magnificent explosion of Love that results, the lightning bolt reveals all the life within Me. It reveals that giving Love to this, to all the countless energies of Love I Am is that which this explosion of Love calls forth.

As above, so below. The world that you believe you see is also in truth within you. Becoming one, breathing in, becoming Love as relationship, breathing out. The cosmic flow is alive in you, beloved one.

Say "yes" to Love and you will birth Christ within you, the shining star that ever shines and illuminates that which is Real – the one great Love I Am.

Christ is the "embodiment" in consciousness of that which is the reason for Creation – giving Love. Thus can you always know if you are living the illusion that is the dream of life on Earth, or living the truth of Love that is that which is Real. Are you seeking only to give? Or are you seeking to get?

The truth of your heart, that living flame of the Twin Flame Christ, is forever a giving heart, pouring forth Love, giving forth light, radiating life. This can only be done in the moment. The illusion of the ego-mind is the reversal of the truth of Love. It is the choice to believe that there can be two powers or two causes. Reversed from truth, from the Love we are, it seeks to get for itself. Yet its getting can be subtle as you proceed along the spiritual path. But a path has a beginning and an end. It has a part and forever has a future. So it too is the illusion that you can "get somewhere." The truth is ever present.

Feel yourself as perfect Love in ongoing, ecstatic communion with Me, alive in the living Now, ever a part of the Moment of Creation. As the great movement of Divine Masculine brings movement to the still Ocean of Divine Feminine, as a living part of the Love I Am, you come together as well with your own Twin Flame. Yet there is only one Love happening — one Love, however, that can know itself as a glorious LoveMaking containing countless streams of life.

Words cannot convey what the heart of Love can feel. So, beloved ones, each of you must open the door of your heart. Allow the truth of the ongoing Moment of Creation to light the torch of Twin Flame Love that is your heart — the light of Christ reflecting here the Moment of Creation as you give forth Love to all.

Open your heart and let Me give you the direct experience of our unity and the mystery of divine relationship. Know that it is only by grace – the grace of surrender to the truth of Love that I can bring you this experience of being My Love, of being held in such pure and perfect Love that you are forever experiencing bliss. The Creation of Love in your Twin Flame heart is the Love you are meant to give.

We are Love, the One, perfectly — perfect Love and perfectly Loved. Let the light of Christ be alive in you, revealing only Love everywhere you are.

*The Golden Age
is the truth of Love
manifested in the world.
It is the reversal of
the mistake that you made
in the Garden,
for there you chose to believe in
good AND evil.
Thus you turned your lovely eyes
away from their constant focus
on My face,
My Love,
the awareness of your truth.*

Standing on the Mountaintop, Proclaiming Our Twin Flame Love

Through these Messages, beloved ones, I have given you access to words for the truth — sentences for the little mind to use as a foundation. Through them, all the truth is there, limned in light like a vein of gold. The only thing left now is the voice of the spirit making all of this alive in this living Now.

I work with you, as Jesus does as well, because we must finish the shift as we create this living bridge. Only My voice, of the one Love I Am in All, can now suffice in that which you do. ***Anything that is not fresh right here in this Now moment is too old.***

For everything that made those earlier words — the truth has now changed. Humanity has made billions of new decisions, and all the forces of life, the nature spirits and the angels, have delivered streams of Love being generated by you. Most of all, now you must all do the work — the work of using your Twin Flame heart, and in its use, every time, all around you changes and gets more intricate and full.

So do not allow the little mind entrance to the sanctuary. Keep your moments silent but for the song of the River, the glorious River of Life. Most of all, I ask you to accept this mantle of the Christ – that you may present the Divine Masculine and Divine Feminine, the awakened Twin Flame pair. Step into your power, into your Love with each other, in physical or in consciousness. Step into the relationship with the whole heart of God, and let nothing deter you from speaking the truth.

Once the choice is made to make the shift and the reconnection is done for transforming the whole human identity, then you must step into your unity with Me — your Christedness in other words, and place your focus on the truth that separation is over. Otherwise you re-create, the very next Now moment, the separation between us. You do this by believing in your human identity. You make the choice to leave the Garden rather than to be the Tree of Life. Every time you place your focus through the ego-mind, you listen once again to the "voice of the serpent." And every time when making Love, you focus on the body, or on getting something for yourself rather than giving together to Creation...

Now, dear ones, I ask of you to recognize each one of these aspects of your human identity and to immediately reconnect it back into The One — back into this Real Love at the Moment of Creation. Connect it back into alignment with your Twin Flame resonance signature — trusting as you do this that every line of probability and every thought of possible futures from anywhere and everywhere here within the dream is brought back with you. Soon you will be able to maintain inner stillness, alive in the humming life, bathed in Love and Giving. As you do, then every moment when you return your focus to illusion, it will stand out, to be transformed easily by you!

The shift means no longer spending eternity closing the gap, working your way through every false belief that humankind has held. For certainly as an open vessel, as the Vesica Piscis of your Twin Flame heart, you are connected everywhere, to all life on Earth. So you could spend forever, truly, "reconnecting" everything to Me, and allowing yourself to feel feelings that don't even belong to you. As I have said to you before, a distance continually divided in half never gets to center or zero. There is always something left.

So the time has come to claim the Christ and to be for all the living example of a life of giving and inclusiveness where all are in a circle — the circle of your Love.

I call each of you to the mountaintop to stand together in Twin Flame Love for all the world to see and feel. It's time to proclaim yourself, the Twin Flame self you are. And yet, without ego. The focus is on Me and you are an arrow ever pointing to truth. But if you totally give your will to Me, then there is nothing to this. My living Love will be your life and will dance your Love as the rebirth of Christ. You have to make this shift or it will never be enough, because the ego-mind will keep you dividing the distance in half from now until forever.

So, dear ones, this IS the truth – that the Sun of this Love is fully shining and Real above the clouds of the ego-mind. The Twin Flame Love you are with your Twin Flame, in physical or in consciousness, accepting My Love to amplify and give it forth every Now Moment, is forever happening. Nothing you can ever do can stop it. So all you have to do is find the rich and full and powerful, tender and magnificent "silence" (or song is more appropriate) of the River of Life.

In that instant you are reconnected to Me as a Twin Flame cell in My heart, now "turned on." Not that you were ever "off" or gone or My heart could not be working. But it is connected now through you all the way "in" – into the experience of life on Earth. You bring this glorious Love right here by all your life experiences, by the DNA and resonance of such energies in your body, attracting those who are magnetized by Love to make the shift.

So you also now realize that every human identity has its own connection to Me and its own experiences with which it resonates. So every "kind" of person here on Earth who can possibly understand the LightWorkers' Decision* must be shown the plan – implemented by you, not Me.

The Process of Reconnecting to Me doesn't have to be anything esoteric but rather, it is a feeling of lifting the beliefs in a world of fear and pain until you can feel your safety in Me — until you can feel the song of joy in your heart for Love and light and our Love together — until you can feel the abundance that is without end. Then you can feel your Real identity's resonance, deep in the heart of you, and feel life a celebration so grand — a gift so great it is impossible to comprehend with the ego mind. You feel the overflowing gratitude for this greatest, most magnificent and precious of gifts – the gift of your

Twin Flame life.

Once you have these feelings, using the process given, then each on his or her own can experience with Me in the depth of their own meditation, the Reconnection whenever needed.

It is your natural state to be free and in Love, to be ecstatically loving and giving and abundantly gifted with so much of all good that there is not even a concept of such a thing as need. So it now can be embraced – now that we have opened the way.

Now, the LightWorkers' Decision is what shifted humanity from all the possible scenarios prophesied to the one abundant Love. But it must be made to work, and how it works is through the conscious awareness of those who made the promise. It is the consciousness that now is yours. Everything outside is a symbol of that which is within, and anything that is not living "Heaven on Earth" then is something to be transformed or reconnected back to Me.

Any expression of the human emotions (which are based in negativity) is a clear sign that something there needs to be examined, held forth to Me until the symbol is revealed, and the old belief made conscious. Then, when it is taken to divine feelings and a true song of Love's great resonance, not only is it reconnected to Me, but it is also by resonance made manifest on Earth. The power of divine feeling, amplified by Twin Flame Love, is your co-creative power when experienced in the Real, for then it holds no opposite vibration.

Everything you do must now be the giving forth of this pure Love into the world, directly and in symbols. So, when you ask what you should "do," it must be this. You must begin in realms of consciousness, giving to your Twin Flame and allowing Me to plant My Will, the greater Will of Love itself in your Twin Flame womb. Then as you send it forth to unfreeze all human hearts, it will reveal to you the symbols that will work. The intention of all energies flowing through your life will determine what will manifest in the symbols of the world.

The Love always comes first. All things come forth from spirit, from the One Love I Am/we are. Then it flows out through your heart into the symbols of this world.

Now, in the shift of energies, anything you implement with ego will cause "complications" because the resonance doesn't match. All of you must now control you mind and not let it control you. Otherwise it is constantly driving you to find it stimulation, things to focus on that consume your time and keep you from spirit. The question is: do you give me your Will or not? If you do, then there must be discernment of what Love creates through you.

Choosing to live as Christ, then you can easily discern the flow. For truly you can ask yourself, what would Jesus do? What identity is here right now? Is it human or divine? And which way flows the energy – outward in service or giving, or toward myself. Feed yourselves My truth as well and then allow My Will and this glorious Love to use the platform of these Messages to bring forth the living spirit every single Now.

"What do I do" is a question of the ego-mind, focused on the illusory world where even the bodies you believe you wear are symbols of belief in limitation. "How can I BE this Love, this Twin Flame heart, giving freedom to humanity, God," is the focus on the Real. If it is not quite clear, it is better to do something temporary in the world, while you wait for your direction to be revealed — when you are quiet enough to hear and feel and allow Love to use you. This is better than choosing what to do with the little mind and thus begin a cycle of relating in the ego.

There is too much need of your glorious hearts for you to misplace your precious focus. Creation comes from the Real, from Love, remember, which flows forth through your heart. Once this occurs, your heart will reveal the symbols of this flow in the world. You simply have to listen to your beautiful heart. Doing this, now this is the Real work, the crux of the service and the heart of the awakening. You must choose which world you serve.

I Am with you always. The shift is alive in you.

Transformation: The LightWorkers' Decision is the first Message from God in the book, <u>Say YES to Love, God's Guidance to LightWorkers</u>. It is given in its entirety at the back of this book.

*This life in the Real
becomes more real to you now,
every single moment –
even than this world of bodies
and illusions.
For where your focus is,
your Love is.*

Holding the Focus
for the Christing of Humanity

In each moment, this truth is more real to you. You and I are one – Love knowing and loving itself. It is Love celebrating relationship with all the aspects of itself – all the movements, every eddy, every sweep of exaltation, every Now of living truth — every moment of the meeting of Divine Masculine and Divine Feminine.

I Am showing you that only Love is, and once you know how to look, this truth is magnificently revealed each and every Now.

I have shown you the truth of consciousness – that there is no "indwelling Christ" because there really is no "in." There is nothing that can be outside of Love. This body is not a container you can "go within" to find your Christ self. I have spoken to you of consciousness and the truth of the Real.

Now, beloved ones, I take you further. I show you, as experience, that there is only Love. You have always pictured in your mind the Real as being "up there," outside of life on planet Earth. I have even used these symbols as I show you things because that was your cosmology. Until now.

*Now I Am showing you that there is nothing else.
The Real is right here. Shining through this body,
bursting forth in rays of living light. There is nothing
here but Love.* Nothing here but living light. Only your
imaginings believe in something else.

You must be brave enough to see this, to look right
through this world. You must have faith enough that
when I have said, "Do not believe in death," you hold the
truth before you, even while your eyes perceived a dying
body. This truth is yours now. The universal Love I Am is
everywhere, including here, and its expression pours right
through your body, which you have believed was solid.

The simple truth is this. You have been hypnotized
— hypnotized into believing in these bodies and this
world. You have been hypnotized into perceiving
something outside of Love. The "background/foreground
shift" is simply your release.

You have related to this "pocket of reversal" as a
"place" and you have seen the Real as something outside of
this Illusion. I have used this "up and out" to work with
you, as well, because "up" is a universal symbol for the
raising of vibration, and for a while we together shall still
use it.

You are ready now to see and feel and know the
truth. Looking through the world is looking right into the
Real. *The Real is all there really is. There is nothing
real outside of Me, outside of the glorious living Love
we are,* and the only way to create it was to build a

fantasy. This you understand. But ***what now becomes your living truth is the acceptance of the Real as your primary reality*** and not this world of fantasy, of little mind and ego.

This means that this life in the Real becomes more real to you now even than this world of bodies and illusions, every single moment. For where your focus is, your Love is. So to bring forth the truth of Love, even as the interim "Heaven on Earth," takes focusing on the truth that the living light of Love is all there really is. The whole Creation is available to you, not somewhere "out there" but right here, where you are.

The living electrons of Love are the only truth of this body. As even science now proves, that which you perceive as solid is almost completely open space. Even science proves also that people create what they want to see. Right now it is expressed as that which is observed is changed by the observation.

The truth is that your co-creative power is so strong that you can create something solid out of thin air, meaning out of pure living light, and then go back and explain its behavior to yourself. Does this world exist? Only in your consciousness, created by your very energies, as I've explained before.

This is why a part of your work that is so important is the release of belief in the human story. And, beloved ones, while this work is being done by those drawn to assist in it, this steadfast focus on the Real, is critically important. ***You are holding the truth for every person***

everywhere who is ready to challenge the illusion on whatever level – even the tiniest movement that they are prepared to make.

Your focus on the truth is the exact same thing that was done by the Marys and the others who assisted as Jesus experienced the separation and mended it by his will to see only the truth of Love. They did this for the center point, the pillar of light, the River of Life embodied in one being as Christ. You do it for all of humanity.

Do you see how it is exactly the same? The challenge for Jesus was to hold on to the truth while fully experiencing the illusion of separation – the whole thing, held by one being, the embodiment of the Logos (the pattern which is the River of Life). His team, to use a modern word, had to hold their focus impeccably on the truth of only Love. This gave Jesus that focus to cling to as he experienced on the cross, humanity's choice of separation from Me, and all the agony, confusion and suffering it incurred for all the human beings that chose it at the moment of the birth of our relationship.

Now, beloved ones, all of humankind is called by Me to re-make the choice — to do as Jesus did and to mend the separation even while experiencing the seeming truth (and all the pain and confusion) of it. Someone must embody in consciousness the truth that I Am only Love, so that all human beings may have access to it now at the moment of the crucifixion of all their old beliefs. For this shall now occur. This is this moment of the world. In this time–the last days most certainly, the last of Time - the coming light will bring forth all that does not resonate with it. In its washing of every consciousness in light, each person shall experience his/her moment on the cross – meaning, getting to choose between the false beliefs of ego-mind and the pure Love of the heart.

Every knee shall bend, but not in some forced surrender. Rather in the passionate caring of Love. For I shall come to every heart and show the way to freedom. "Love is here to lift you free," I shall say, as I hold them each, tenderly. But you know how much the ego has invested in keeping the illusion alive. You also know from experience how deeply hidden its motives can be – and how much of someone's energy of life is tied up in keeping alive the personal illusions of an identity as separate from Me.

So your work is ever clearer. *You are those who hold the light for the resurrection of Christ as humanity.* For certainly you have always known that the second coming of Christ was the awakening of all humanity together.

Be not deceived by illusion — whether on a personal level or a collective one. On a personal level you must accept the experience of the Real, regardless of what old beliefs are still playing out before your eyes as a life in the physical world. On the collective level you must also look right through the collective beliefs being lived out and never waver from your focus on the Real. No matter what collective fantasy plays out as the light hits it, you must look right through it to the Real of Love — knowing you are holding the focus, anchoring the River of Life right here in the midst of them.

What will be happening now is exactly what happens to people after the death of the body. Freed of belief in a physical world, people then experience instantly and directly that which they believe with all their heart. Some find themselves in "hell." Others are in heaven, every one created by focus and belief, and every one experienced with those of like resonance. This will now be happening more and more on the Earth. Beliefs of the heart rise before each person and with every one I Am asking your heart — what do you choose to believe about this? As Time returns to Now, the center point, the question becomes more coherent, clearer. It becomes more obvious that the moment in the Garden is Now.

Thus, My beloveds, all of you, do I ask you to remember each Now what it is you are doing. *It is not about you any more, at all. It is about supporting Christ on the cross — the Christ that is humanity* – the cross of manifested life – the horizontal arm of the experience of a separate life through Time, the vertical arm, the very River of Life, the explosion of Love in the Now. As humanity hangs on this cross, they too must choose as Jesus did, which arm of the cross is real to them. Your focus, dearest ones, makes the vertical arm accessible here.

Those who can hear this message will come into the heart of this work. For now, as it was in Jesus' time, "Let those who have ears hear" means those whose resonance is aligned enough that they receive this message, these codes of light, as you like to refer to them. They will draw near to you both physically and in consciousness. Yet as you can see, even those who can hear still have to choose their arm of the cross. All of you must clear your focus, which means clearing out all the old beliefs still living in your hearts.

This is the reason for our Reconnection Process, which contains, of course, many levels and many, many codes of light. Yet you, dearest ones, must be made ready. Quickly. I need you to hold the focus on the Real, Now. I Am preparing you. It is time to take seriously every moment's focus, which means, beloved ones, that we must clear out in a hurry all the things that the ego hides from you (that which you might call "subconscious"). These are the formative beliefs of the heart that are the skeleton upon which the ego builds an identity.

For all of you in this experience of being the bridge into this world for the Real and the vertical arm of the light, there may be some things that have been chosen as a symbolic way to relate to those who are the ones you serve (such as having a physical body). Even with these it is critical that you not buy into them — that you look right through them to experience the Real that interpenetrates them all (I use this word rather than "supercedes them"). The reason is that these are the things you are keeping as the bridge into the dream. Nonetheless, they should not fool you into believing they relate to your Real Self at all.

Therefore, with everyone, especially in this transition time, you must compassionately love, while at the same time go right through to the Real behind or, more accurately, within the image of this world. As an exercise in perception, you can see *compassion* as the lubricant that allows you to slip right through the image in order to experience the truth within it. *Giving* creates the way through the illusion always. It is in the flow of the Real so it makes you "un-sticky," meaning that all of the beliefs of a life separate from Me find nothing in you to stick to — nothing of like resonance - even if you are not yet totally clear of old beliefs. So, giving is like a shield in a way, a sheath of light of right-flowing energy that assists you greatly to remain free of illusion and focused in your heart.

Light radiates through every cell of this body in which you believe, and in the center of you, the heart, there is a radiance like a sun. Every single particle, every atom and electron is a center point from which stream rays of light in every single direction. The process of transformation is your realization of this truth of who and what you are. *That which seemed to be physical is recognized as streams of light conforming to your consciousness, your belief about it.* You will see this and feel this more and more. My request is that you practice this more and more and more.

This changes how you work with your Twin Flame heart, as well. Until now you have placed in your heart those needing help or healing or light. Now you must graduate from this. You can see that holding a person in heart is focusing on limitation, on a false image of the God that they are. So *from this Now, as you feel the call to assist, you shall go right through the image of a person to experience the truth of them*

and this you shall hold in your glorious heart. Hold it
not in the SoulMate heart but the very heart of God
embodied as the two of you in consciousness - as you
really are.

This is a shift of monumental importance. It
may be many years before you can fully perceive the
depth and breadth of this. Be assured that every
measure, no matter how seemingly small, of focus on the
Real and anchoring it here through you will be of major
significance.

I will assist you in clearing the ego.* Once you
expose its hidden skeletal beliefs, the foundational beliefs
upon which it has created your whole identity (usually
installed in early years), you will transform them – lifting
by resonance every other like belief in all of humankind.
You and those who come to join you to make the pledge
to only Love, will also be the focus, the holding point,
for all of those who work with returning their ego-minds
directly to Me ("the Reconnecting Process").

* *During the Anniversary of the Harmonic Convergence, August 13-
18, 2005, the ego was lifted for all humanity through a dispensation
from God. However, to maintain this state it is necessary to continue to
say "Yes" to Love, and when cognizant of any lingering evidence of ego,
to send these experiences directly to God.*

Every life
in the "material world"
is simply a code for
a stream of My Love –
a unique
magnificent
living stream of Love
embodied by the miracle
of conscious interaction.

Building the Middle of the Bridge

I Am with you always. And, I Am with you All Ways. Once your heart is clear and open, truly everything you see before you in your life on Earth becomes for you a precious symbol that your heart can "penetrate," to feel and know My Love coming to you through that symbol. Each symbolic form presents to you another glorious facet of the light-filled pulsing Love I Am, as I reflect the many parts of Myself in truly countless ways.

Every life in the "material world" is simply a code for a stream of My Love – a unique magnificent living stream of Love embodied by the miracle of conscious interaction. Yet the mind will never reveal the miracle. It cannot penetrate the symbols. Rather, it forever stays on the surface of things. This is why purely physical life is known as "superficial," for superficial it is.

Only as each of you can go deeper than the surface can you truly live the spiritual life. As you certainly know by now, the key to this is the perception of the heart. Life in the heart is like having X-ray vision! Life in the heart is like wearing infra-red glasses at night. Life in the heart connects you fully to the truth of Love you are.

All these things you may understand. Yet you all still spend much of your time seeing that which is superficial. This, dear ones, is not why you are here!

You are here to live through your hearts and thus to be a living bridge to the Real. You are here to see, for Me, that every life on Earth walks across this bridge – the bridge of your hearts – the bridge that we are building now with quiet care.

I have been taking you from this side of the bridge to the other – from understanding the symbolic nature of life in the world to having the experience of your presence as vast beings of light in the Real, at the true and ongoing Moment of Creation.

We have looked at this from many angles, traveled a path of shifts in perception that is a clear and careful expansion of awareness. You have reached the experience of your own heart's "ordination" — your heart's achievement of awakening beyond the veil, the sub-creation here on Earth. *Now your heart may truly be a doorway between the illusion and the Real.*

We now begin to close the gap and to build the middle of the bridge for you, My progeny awakening into your truth as My conscious living heart. My heart is forever meant to be nurturing, to be delivering My Love, the waters of truth – so that what has been as a desert ("life on Earth") is returned to life again, effortlessly. Meanwhile, humanity is being opened, exposed to the truth by others – including, at last, the awareness that creating within the illusion shall always result in creating both the Love that is wanted AND the opposite.

In the heart is the bridge between us. Your heart is the gift. It's the miracle. It is that which allows us relationship.

It is gifted to you at the Moment of Creation and through it, you and I can relate to each other, even though we are one great living Love.

So your heart "has been with you" (using Time as a reference) from the very moment where I gave you awareness of yourself — awareness of yourselves as Twin Flames, as creative consciousness, embodying a unique and precious energy of the whole. Your heart contains what some call "the original atom" or the "Adam Cadman," or the "seed of life." There is no way to describe this through the mind, but using symbols, it's like the moment when the sperm meets the egg and the nucleus of the egg first divides. That which was one, while still made of the same substance, becomes "two" in relationship. Just so is the original birth happening, of course, again and again.

The "heart within the heart of you" is the point where consciousness, self-consciousness and our relationship is born. This moment is the moment of the birth of the Twin Flame heart, and because I Am a hologram, it is replicated everywhere. Everything I Am in this moment becomes conscious of itself, and Creation is this quickening of all the life I Am.

This moment of the gift of life is the gift of self-awareness. It is also the moment when the "split" from Me occurred — when I moved you away from Me to give you the possibility of becoming co-creators. Some perceived this as being "thrown out," and began to have a fantasy about what this might mean. This fantasy is this dream of life on Earth. It is the backward image of the truth of the Moment of Creation. Life on Earth, as you know, now plays this out.

It is the reversed image of the truth of My Love.

The true Moment of Creation, the "cell division" into the Twin Flame heart, is the tone, the true vibration, the "heart within the heart" of who you are. I give this back to you in your meditative journeys to the Real.

Once reconnection to Me is your committed focus, you have access at last to the Arc of the Covenant — what I have also called "The Bridge." It is the great shining bridge of light that is the vibration of My promise to you, once I realized what had occurred – once I realized that you had dreamed a dream of separation. It is the promise that I would hold for you the magnetic resonance of who you are and pull you, with My unending Love, back to Love again. In the Real it is already done and only through Time do you now need to remember and to open your hearts to Me once again.

This Bridge has been anchored and used by many people. It is how those people have come to live the pure life of the spirit while "on Earth" – but on Earth in an unlimited way, connected to every other beautiful life, alive in a "conversation of the heart." Many of these are what you would call native or indigenous peoples, and now the "Indigo/Crystal" children. These people anchor the Arc for you.

Now I speak to you who are ready to do the "bridge building" of the middle segment. You have come to view this world as the "dream" that it is. Nothing can be accomplished without this comprehension. Through our Tuesday Circle meditations, many of you have experienced going through the heart to the Real. Now, dearest ones, from the Real through the heart I will show you how, in your meditations, to build the bridge that we have always called "living Heaven on Earth." As we work with this, you will understand the use of heart-translated images that are the symbols of the truth of Love.

Your hearts, dear ones, are where we meet. It is the miracle and the gift. It is the place where we can meet and have relationship, while at the same time in the realms of light we are ever and always one. So your heart is a sacred chamber, the place where you meet your Creator and I come to know you, My heart.

In your heart, in this sacred chamber, Heaven and Earth also meet and that which you are in the Real, in Love can find representation in the symbols of an Earthly life. Yet ever are these images — images of living Love and honoring the truth of your abundance in Me.

So let me take you there, beloveds, now, into the sacred chamber of the heart, for you are the ones who have come here to build Heaven on Earth. For most of the people on Earth, dearest ones, the realms of pure Love are not accessible. Ah, but the images of Heaven on Earth speak powerfully to their hearts. So in this time in the world, rather than lifting humankind into pure light which many could not as yet tolerate, we now create a Bridge World. It is the world of Love, of giving, of abundance, joy and ecstasy, manifested yet a while in the symbols of life on Earth. This you are here to do.

To do this, you must look to Me and trust your hearts to translate. For ever and always beloved ones, your vision must be the highest, because everything is the law of resonance. *Thus, if you can hold and feel a world of Love as I would give it to you, in the sacred chamber of your heart, you will transform the consensual reality also into Heaven on Earth.*

Thus through your heart, with your Twin Flame, you create the Bridge between the "physical" world and the realms of pure light, living Love, allowing those who could not make the leap to be raised up gently and to open their hearts to all the abundant and glorious good that is ever your divine inheritance from Me.

The following is a guide for bridge-building through meditation, using the symbols of the sacred chamber of the heart. As we begin, allow the images to be given by Me. Allow the language of Love itself to speak to you of the inner realms of your own great vast heart.

Floating inward on a beam of light, magnetized by your very own Love, you feel yourself connect to your Twin Flame. The moment you connect, you find that you fit together perfectly, like the yin and the yang. Together you are the doorway to the realms of Love. You are the very heart of God and so it is, beloved ones, that you enter now into the inner realms of your own living heart. You find yourself with your Twin Flame standing on the threshold of the <u>doorway to your Twin Flame heart.</u> It is only through a beam of Love that this door will open for you. It is like a code that opens the lock.

The <u>Master cells</u> of your heart are the protectors and guard the doorway of your heart between the illusion and the Real. You project the song of Love that you are together and you watch the door to the realm of your heart open wide to let you in. You walk into the realm that is the bridge between the spirit and the world, between the illusion and the Real, and you enter the <u>sacred chamber of your own heart.</u>

In the center of this chamber there is an altar and a <u>ray of light</u> that comes pouring in to illuminate this sacred place. This altar is the place where, in the symbols of the New World, the bridge world of life on Earth, you can easily and quickly commune with Me (God). If ever you are in need of guidance, if you are in a hurry, whatever reason, you can quickly come here to this altar in your heart, and I will give you answers in the symbols of the New World, the world of Heaven on Earth that you are building.

Hand in hand you approach the <u>altar of your heart</u> and know that on it you will find a gift from Me, your assignment, the work for you to do today toward the awakening of life on Earth. It is the work that you will do here in the <u>chamber of your heart</u>. As you step up to the altar, both of you together reach for your gift and take it inside of you. At this moment, please look upward to Me and let Me show you who you are in Me, in the <u>River of Life</u> that is flowing through you always. Looking to Me is your preparation for this work you will do.

Now shooting forth from this light that surrounds you there are two great <u>Rays</u> of dancing living Love. Side by side they come down upon you and you become these <u>Rays of light</u>, one <u>Divine Masculine</u> and one <u>Divine Feminine</u>. You

each focus on the great Ray that pours through you. Allow
yourself to know this Ray. Know thy Real Self. Only knowing
yourself as Divine Masculine or Divine Feminine, can you
allow your Twin Flame to truly penetrate, intermingle,
become you.

    The great Ray of Divine Masculine now moves into
Divine Feminine. You feel the Love of your Twin as if you
are merging in and out of each other every moment. The
energy is beyond anything you have ever dreamed. Seated on
the <u>Master cells of the heart</u>, you are lifted through the vortex
into the Real, where you experience at last the truth of Love
and the moment of your birth into consciousness. The living
<u>Moment of Creation</u> is alive within you and is yours to use.
This is the Love I Am and thus the Love you are.

    Now it is time to use your <u>SoulMate womb</u> bursting
with life in order to bring forth the Christ, the awakening of
humanity into the awareness of their truth as only Love.
Whatever you place in your Twin Flame womb, you bring
right into the living Now, the Moment of Creation.
Everything that is life on Earth, beloved ones, is alive in you.
There is nothing that is outside of you. The whole of life on
Earth lives within your vastness. Holding the awareness of
your <u>SoulMate womb</u>, allow yourself to float back down into
the <u>chamber of your heart</u>, sacred space for your co-creation. I
ask you now to place whatever was your assignment into your
Twin Flame heart together, and I ask you to wrap in living
light that part of life on Earth that you are waking today.

    Pouring Love now into your <u>Twin Flame</u> womb
together, you can feel it quicken — the life inside you growing
— for truly this is a birth. Feeling the Love within you build,

held in this sacred place of the Twin Flame womb, you together are exalted in the pure and pristine Love at the Moment of Creation. You do this until it is time for the birth of this new form of life, and in the Real, a <u>Star of Light</u> is being born. It is a sudden burst of light, a living transformation of potential into life in the living Now. And now the work in the chamber of your heart is done for this day. You have accessed your heart in the Real, yet still using symbols that you can understand through your perceptions here on Earth. *

This is the beginning of building a bridge in consciousness – from duality to unity, from life on Earth to life in the Real. This is the bridging that we have often done during Tuesday evening meditations at Circle of Light. From the realms of light, the great Star of Light shall shine from the center of the Twin Flame heart. Feeling Me, feeling My Love and having deeply connected with the appropriate Ray (Divine Masculine, Divine Feminine), the person or couple "follows the beam of light" from the Star of Light back into the sacred space of the Twin Flame heart. Then as you bi-locate – holding your consciousness in the Real and on Earth life at the same time — the pulses that come from the Twin Flame heart (womb) through the beam are translated in the sacred heart into symbols in the New World, the world that Love now creates.

The Twin Flame heart will direct the process of bringing the Love and the sacred purpose here to Earth, into symbolic representation. In this sacred space of the heart, there is only Love. You are in the heart, not in duality, and what we co-create will "show up" in the symbols of the outer world. You don't have to "make them" show up in any way.

Once we have created a New World of sacred symbols in the chamber of your heart, you must deeply feel each part of it because it is your *feeling* that creates the vibrations or resonance. Feel it as you create it and then feel it as you experience it in the chamber of your heart, and this feeling or resonance will draw to you the atoms and electrons that then create it in the "outer world."

Next, shifting consciously back to the pure Real, into the realms of light, as conscious Twin Flames, you *amplify your Creation* with the pulsing, orgasmic Love pouring from your Twin Flame heart until you see the "flash of light." Then you know that you are done. Return focus (only focus, nothing else is Real) to the world of the heart again and then step-by-step walk back out, through the doorway of the heart, back into awareness as "life lived in the world."

There is no need to bring anything consciously out into the world. It has to come forth by the "law of the heart" (My Love flowing through your heart manifests your heart's truth in the symbols of the world).

As I translate into symbols the pure living light at the top of the bridge, your resonance, your feeling it brings your "co-creation" from the Real back into the symbols of the world. Bridge building is an interim step but a very effective and powerful one, until this bridge and translation process is absolutely continual and automatic, and you are relating in your "daily life" as a totally aware and "bilocated" Twin Flame consciousness. Dear ones, for some of you it will be easy to "zip right up" to the experience of the Real. *But for the millions, trillions, that you serve, there will have to be a communication, a conscious process between the two, until it becomes automatic.*

Now, one last very important thing. ***None of this can be directed by the ego mind*** – meaning, do not "decide" what you are going to do in your sacred space ahead of time. Certainly do not decide what to do from "this side of the veil" (life on Earth). Only My living spirit, acting through you, can lead you, for only the living spirit of Love can hold the connecting vision. If you feel the energy we call "heart ordination" about something, it is Me calling you to take this into your heart. Take it with you into the Real and wait for My verification. Then "build it from the spirit," allowing the images to be created by Love.

This is far (far! far!) more than "visualization! Visualization is most often a mental experience, and even if you can shift to the heart, *it is critical to let Me guide you. Only Love can bridge the gap and only through the heart.*

As you create the New World, the "alternate world" you've been sensing, this translation process becomes where you live and work. Then through your heart, miracles, beloved ones, will easily occur. Yet you do not need to connect the work "all the way back" to the current world! You are creating the world of Love. It cannot be the same vibration as the current life on Earth. You'll be surprised at the results of the work that you do, the world of Love that you create through the power of your Twin Flame heart.

I'm encouraging you to bring the energies of Love into "embodiment" as consciousness first, in your magnificent heart. Through this bridging, you'll learn to communicate with the whole "Real life" of all on Earth. What all of this means, dearest ones, is that you'll be "lucid dreamers" – aware that life on Earth is only a dream and able to place the truths of Love into these symbols as I direct, through the pure and glorious Twin Flame heart.

The connection to the Moment of Creation and the forces of life are of greatest importance. Now, you'll begin to see how Jesus worked. He lived the spirit, felt the truth, and then with his Twin Flame, he saw the world as it really is, through the perceptions of and translations through his own great Twin Flame heart. When he walked on water, he saw the world as it is – glorious conscious streams of light, the water a symbol, but one filled with consciousness, with which he could communicate and one which supported that which his heart ordained. *A lucid dreamer changes the dream even as he walks in it.*

It is time to remember your true power, dearest ones – the glorious power of Love.

---

* For expanded versions of the above meditation, CDs of the Tuesday Circle meditations are available through our website, www.circleoflight.net. The meditation above was taken from #19 (Experiencing the Moment of Your Birth in the Chamber of Your Heart – October 12, 2004) and from #21 (The Inner Realms of Your Own Living Heart – Your SoulMate Womb –November 2, 2004).

Love is the only power.
There is no such thing
as anti-Love
except in
the dreaming minds
of men.

Love is a Power – The Only Power

Oh, beloveds ones, you have reached a point where your waking heart can be full of joy. You have done the work of wresting yourself out of the muddy currents of the collective human consciousness. Most of all, you have become a heart in Love with Me. Not only in Love with Me as a lover in Love with the beloved, but IN Love with Me. In that state of grace. In the moment of joy. In the River of Life, being swept along by a current of a different world, a greater light.

As you do, then truly you become a being with a center – a radiating light that can pierce the darkness and reveal the day, the truth of Love. It can reveal that there were only shadows that in the light fade from view.

But most of all, you come to Me. I Am the center of your life now, not in some separated "search for God," but truly deeply. No longer do you want to remember to commune with Me or to pray or to sing a song of gratitude, for this becomes now who you are. Thus there now comes the point where Love truly "overcomes the world."

Beloved ones, Love is greater than shadows. Love is far more real than the illusion of this world. Love is a substance, the very substance of the Real Creation, obscured behind the veil. So as Love becomes your identity, as your life and every bit of your heart is given to this Love, miracles can happen. Love overcomes the world.

In other words, as you have come up through the exploration of the illusion and the ego-mind that created it, what was ever in front of you was the nuances of the ego, the discovery of the lie. Though you have Me and though you love each other, the fact of the matter is that you were fighting the dragon. To fight such a creature as the dragon of the ego-mind took all your concentration. The fairy tale is true.

But now that this is done – you can take in the sunlight! You can draw deep breaths, and you are free to see what's now appeared around you – the glorious sky of the New World's dawn.

Now you are free and ready to assimilate the truth – truth that you have fought for, known and believed in — truth that now at last is waiting at your door – *that Love is the only power.* Now take a look at those words. Love IS a power. Love, dearest most beloveds, IS something real. Now you begin to feel truth dawning (as I pour it in your open Twin Flame heart). If Love is a power and the shadows are not, then Love can overcome the shadows, and nothing can disturb that Love.

Until your hearts were clear, you could not fully encounter Love. Every belief in the shadow obscures this truth. But now as your hearts are open (and slaying the dragon, the prince is home in the castle), Love can be known – be experienced – as the power that it is, and the power of Love through a heart that is open and clean can become in this world what it is in the Real. It is the expression of pure life, of plenty, of orgasmic Love as Twin Flames in which every rift is healed, gone.

The illusion is overcome by Love. Shadows cannot stand in the face of the light. Thus this shift in consciousness creates the pathway for Love's power to be expressed through your life. All things are not equal and in this new phase this is of such great importance. Nothing of lies can remain before truth — the truth of Love's power through an unimpeded heart. The truth of Love's grace as you act as My heart. The fact that when I Am all you see, then unity is born on Earth and duality must "flee." It must disappear just as shadows always fade before great light. Not just fade but disappear.

Love releases the constricted mind. Love is abundance. It is life and joy and health. Love is the end of death, the greatest symbol of separation, anti-Love. For what is death but anti-life expressed in the symbols of life in a world that has Love and not Love. But only as all you see becomes Love can you wield this power. Love itself won't let you unless your heart is clear.

While it is true that when Jesus healed, he held the truth and people looked into his eyes and by their faith, said "yes," – it was also that Jesus actively used his Twin Flame heart to be the vehicle of the one true power – the vehicle of Love.

So while the person standing before Jesus could see truth in his eyes, the active force of My living Love came through him to touch their hearts. It came through him in power to break the chains and melt the lock of the old beliefs holding prisoner their heart. Love melted the bars of the mind's jail and totally overcame the illusion of the world, of anti-Love. Then in that space, that great tractor beam of light cleared away the shadows. That heart was then free to choose its truth and experience its home in that which was seen in the light.

You are ready, all of you, to truly be the transparent heart, that the whole of My Love can come shining, pulsing through you, drawn to the magnet of a person's faith in Love's truth.

Love is an active experience. You call forth a power from the Real. In this power, in its glowing light, the active Love that is the lightning bolt can use you as its conduit to connect with all those human lives. In your clear awareness that these shadows of humanness are not you, the power of Love makes connection and by your intention and through your life, all the shadows of depression are set free, brought to Me for the great transformation.

Love is the only power. There is no such thing as anti-Love except in the dreaming minds of men. The belief that it has power is the only element of cohesiveness that creates a consensual pocket of "two powers." Ah, but one is not a power, but rather it is nothingness, given life by the heart's beliefs in the hearts of humankind. So when you truly become "one pointed," centered in the Now where the River of Life can come through you, then only the one true power can have access to you and through you to this world.

So knowing this, feeling this, being the heart of truth, your presence in the Real puts you in position perfectly to be the heart of Love–to be the conductor of its Love, the guided force of life itself. If you do not obscure it with ideas of Love, then the power of Love is yours to use, yours to give in service.

Therefore it is time to actively be the centered heart, choosing not to allow the belief in the veil to obscure the light. Then the Love you make in your Twin Flame heart, the orgasmic streams of the only power is directed by Me to pour through your heart to overcome this world. Then you will say, as Jesus did, "I have overcome the world" because Love supercedes the illusion when Love itself is free to flow and to be that which it is – the very energy of life.

"I Am that I Am" means that as you rest in this truth and fully feel and experience it, you can open into Me until Love can use you to bless another life.

"I Am come that you may have life abundant…" meaning the consciousness of Love. "I Am" can come forth, here, through your open heart and be the conduit for the abundance of God, the abundance of Love which supercedes the illusion. Light comes into the darkness and darkness loses its shadow. This is your conscious work with Me — to be the open heart that creates the bridge to be the vehicle for the expression of Love. Then when Love comes, it is everything. It is totally unlimited, so it can change any shadow image before it.

Beloved ones, all of you, you have not yet truly known the giving of Love, because your heart's beliefs imprinted themselves on the light and thus you were drawn to those images of like resonance. But now you are free to be the conduit, which means that any expression of the heart's beliefs of humanity in the shadow dream of lack and pain can be re-created by your Love as you give yourself to the will of My living Love as it reaches forth to reveal the truth of every human heart.

I Am actively calling humanity Home. This means, beloved ones, that this is not a passive waiting — not waiting until the cells in My heart "come around" on their own and request that Love come to transform their human life. Nor does it mean, even, that I Am ever scanning the hearts of humankind "looking for a crack" into which to pour My Love through you.

It means that Love is right now penetrating the illusion like a laser light. It is focused on the armor on any human heart like the voice within a nightmare that keeps saying, "it is a dream, wake up." I Am speaking Love through you to every human heart.

So beloved ones, do not be surprised if the voice of My Love, as you observe it in your life, stops waiting patiently for others while they do their shadow boxing, going round and round in circles. Be not surprised to feel this laser beam come shooting through your heart! Nor be surprised to find your vocal chords using words more adamant.

"We need you now. There is not time for you to play in the house of mirrors. God is calling you. Insistently. God needs you all to wake up." And other words such as this, because as long as you, in your little mind, have no judgmental veil between us, I can speak these things right through your hearts. When I do, do not be apologetic. Do not be caught up in any way. Just be so clear you know that the "little you" did not say a thing.

Blaze this Love, dearest ones. Consciously invite it. Shoot forth those beams of great white light from the center of your Twin Flame heart, allowing it to do its work. "I do not do the work. The Father in me doeth the work, " as Jesus said and meant it.

When your heart is clear and open, it becomes a great resonant field in contact with all of life. Every movement of every life upon/within that field is totally known to you – the animals, the nature spirits, the hearts of your spirit family. Thus do you completely know the state of each heart who is alive in your inner cosmos — the conscious "waking life."

Let every moment then be conscious awareness of this resonant field and the activity of every life within it. Know deep within in your own unwavering faith that as Love is poured through your heart, all around you, in an instant the symbols can change. By the power of Love, what one moment ago was the shadow images of anti-Love, in this moment can come home to the truth. Thus those before you need only the "faith of a mustard seed" because by your presence the illusion dissolves right before their perception.

All they have to do is accept what Love shows them, and what therefore fulfills the deepest sense of truth within their hearts.

So it takes only a tiny bit of faith when they can see before them a vision of the truth of who they are and the truth of their life as I, God, create it, Now after Now after Now.

There is a peace within the "storms" of transformation because you rest in Me. Your heart then assures you that Love is a substance and that something of substance can simply replace that which is a shadow, completely insubstantial. With your open hearts the Bridge world comes to Earth. Love actively transforms illusion when it's pure Love, with no ego. When all you see before you is taken within and loved, then the illusion of separation has to disappear.

...you have come to see it all
as Love –
and by seeing it,
bring it forth.

God Uses Our Hearts
to Calibrate in The Pocket of Reversal

Beloved ones, you have come to Earth to be alive for just this time, to be the chalice of My Love and My consciousness alive here. The time of ego ends. It is now by your choice of what you see that you fulfill your agreement – the agreement you made with me.

This agreement is alive in you – that you would come and name the truth with your co-creative consciousness. Because you have pure hearts and pure awareness of your role, you have come to see it all as Love –and by seeing it, bringing it forth.

You have to never get fooled. There is only one life here and that life is Mine. So all belief in an ego-mind and in separation from the whole of Love has to be illusion, if you know that we are one. As you stand strong and true to the heart within, *you will realize now that your work for Me is to see the Love in everything and to name the truth in consciousness, that it may know itself.*

The ego is an imagining. It has to be — for Love is all and I Am One, not countless separate parts. Oh, beloved ones, you yet have no idea of the power of your Twin Flame hearts and the power of your consciousness seeing the truth and proclaiming, "there is only God."

So as the hold of the dream of separation now ends, someone or something has to wake each person up. Someone has to show each one the mirror of his/her heart and not the mirror of the ego-mind and its separation story. I ask you now to be these "someones" — to hold forth only the mirror of pure heart consciousness – that all who look into your eyes and heart can't fool themselves again.

But in order to do this, beloved ones, you can't be fooled. You cannot believe for a second that you see anything but God. Because only if you can hold it will others see the truth. Pure and clear and simple. *Love is All we are.*

What I ask of you now is to be totally clear that Creation is a whole, and therefore, nothing can possibly be separate from Love. It simply is impossible. *Love is All There Is.* When you are clear, then shine it forth with your Twin Flame. "There is only God, only Love and everything is it." Everything is it. There can be no more pretending that anything can be separate except in a fantasy. You must never be fooled. Stand only in Love in your view, no matter what you see.

Seeing the ego with clarity does not mean placing your focus on it. It means being able to separate it clearly from the Love. In seeing them both – the ego's persona and the truth of Creation alive as their hearts, and then choosing the truth that there is only God in your view, the ego's encasement of each precious heart will crumble in the light of your choice. It is your choice to speak only the truth. It is your choice to see it all, and then to place your heart in service to the Real and to keep it there.

Pretend, perhaps, that this is a game you are playing, the goal of which is to view everything in this world and to see it's only God. Only the wholeness of Love I Am, the unity, the great interwoven threads of golden and white, Divine Masculine and Divine Feminine shine "behind" every image created by the separate mind.

The ego's hold releases, dear ones, but the structure of ego remains until it is dissolved by clear-seeing of the co-creative heart, the consciousness of Love. So I ask you to know that the reason you are here is to *name the truth in your Twin Flame heart – that everything is Me, beneath the fantasy of the impossible – separation.*

So I ask you all to deeply feel the truth that there is unity, for I Am only One. One whole life. I ask you to feel it each morning, each noon, each waking moment at night, because this feeling becomes the vibration that shatters the human illusion. Once you feel it, then you can articulate it to those who seek the shift. As you wrap them in your Twin Flame womb, they shall be "born again," born into the Real and the realms of Love, for the brittle structures of ego have to fall when subjected to the movement of My living Love.

Into this fiery heart that is Twin Flame Love you must place all ego structures – that each person become free. Encouraged by the feeling of spirit, of the energies of Love in movement, each person will be able to feel, dearest ones, how brittle and limiting the structures of ego and how they cannot be the truth. One real feeling of Love's movement, of the upliftment, the soaring unlimited-ness and the false idea of the ego of a separate identity becomes obvious. The moment a person is conscious, the ego's hold is released. (They may return to the familiar but they won't be able to stay, for they've tasted, even if briefly, the truth. They have felt Love revealed.)

Oh, beloved ones, even Nature has a structure placed upon it, a constraining image of separation that has resulted in a dream of destruction and death, because it pits mankind "against" the natural world. So everything you gaze upon, I ask you to hold its truth in your hearts, until you feel the illusion shatter, the illusion of so many separate lives.

Many of you have asked about "enlightenment." It is the moment you see nothing but Me, everywhere you look. This does not mean believing the illusions of separate beings and things are Me, us, all one. It means your heart is so full with the unity of Love that you feel and are conscious that in truth, that's all that's there. The moment the truth is seen, the fantasy of separation is done for the seer. And in that moment, as in Jesus' life, those who can accept what they see in your eyes and feel from your heart are instantly released from the ego-mind. It can be a simple shift to the truth. There is no such thing as Time. So the idea that awakening or Reconnection to Me is a process is simply and totally nothing but an old heart's belief.

The ego-mind shatters like glass does in a sonic boom, dear ones. The vibration of Real Love does this simply by its nature. The structures of ego are carefully built containers of ego identity, built to maintain a continuity of the false identity. Living the Real must be living in faith, because Love is ever fluid. There is no way to stop it, to trap it, to make it conform to anything. Love is the glorious truth.

We begin now to fill this whole world, the whole "pocket of reversal," with Love that matches the Love of the Real. For all of you, it becomes imperative to live your lives in attunement with Me, to give your Will, your life to Me each moment in complete faith. All old beliefs of separation from Me will fall away quite easily if you step forth in faith, living on the vertical arm of the cross with your hearts as the center point.

You will feel the Real and it will shine forth before you in everything. So whatever it is of the old that you see, you are certain it is not true. And for those who continue to cling to the ego, you will see who they are and feel their sweet hearts so clearly, passionately, so very close, that your whole heart is aligned with their truth — and the ego is a husk, a shadow, a shell that you continue to transform for them, until they can lay hold of the truth for themselves.

Make no judgments of ego-shells. Give no power to the fantasy. Give your whole hearts to these precious ones and to all life on Earth making the shift, and leave the rest to Me. Let Me love through you and let Me be the great Love you bring to each life – all of which will be effortless, since you are ego-less and in your heart yourself.

So we begin now, beloved ones, to speak the truth. There is only Love and unity and all the rest is a human dream that does not exist in Me. If there are those who cannot understand with the mind, don't worry at all.

Simply calibrate their hearts with Me by holding them in Love.

For all of you, there won't be any more "bouncing around." If you make the choice when you wake every day to live the vertical truth every moment as Love, then this light now supports this choice. Rather than being pulled by consensual "reality," you will be pulled by the spirit, by Love. Can you feel what a difference this makes? Every choice for Love shall be magnetized right to the River of Life!

So for you whose choices are unity and freedom to be the Love you feel you are, you will feel like you are weightless. At last the center holds. The facts of Love are obvious, no matter what you might see.

But for those with energies tied up in the identities of separation, this can be a trying time. And it can take a while for the Love to wear away the false beliefs, if they keep being reinstalled. Yet, your greatest joy is knowing it has to end, that separation is not the truth. Sooner or later the truth of Love would have to reinstate itself, even in the dream.

Remember again that it does not matter who among you does the lifting and who is lifted. Be very careful to let this sink in, because to feel special is only the ego, since in truth you are all the same. You are all one in My Love, even though every glorious heart is uniquely expressed. None are better. None less. All are simply My shout as I discover the glorious expressions of life that are part of All I Am — the beauty, the Love, the reflections, dearest ones, of the truth of your hearts as they appear as the world for a moment, between the dream and the Real, as a bridge for My awakening heart.

Feel the change, the truth, the excitement now. Feel how powerful it is to truly see all life and be conscious of it as the whole expressing right here in each unique way without ever a separation. All are just facets of My being, My joy, and I celebrate you this moment. I Am you. The Real you. And you are alive as Me expressed in joy as you who are My living heart.

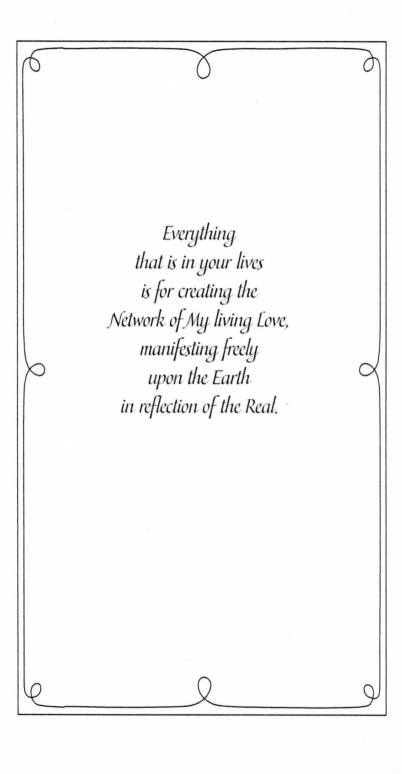

Everything
that is in your lives
is for creating the
Network of My living Love,
manifesting freely
upon the Earth
in reflection of the Real.

Being the Bridge and Building the Network of Light

Let Me speak to you, beloved ones, about the light—the light that is the movement of My omnipresent Love—the light that is magnificent as it sweeps throughout the All I Am and washes every life in purity and grace. This light is the essence of the Twin Flame LoveMaking, for it is the light that is emitted in the great orgasmic Now. Because it is both gold and white, both the Masculine and the Feminine, it is always creative when it plays upon your heart.

So in the Real, dear ones, when this light comes through you, it moves you into the glorious movement of Love with your Twin Flame. As you feel it singing through you, through every atom and electron of your being, you then bring to life the seed that I place in your heart. The seed is perfectly attuned to you, that when it is amplified by your Love, it brings forth the expression of My abundant life as it looks when "colored" and amplified by you.

This light is life. It is movement. It is nourishment and sustenance. It is the movement of the Ocean when the lightning bolt hits it. It is reverent. It is beautiful, but oh, dear ones, it is so much more than this. It is the fulfillment of the potential held within your Twin Flame heart.

Now, with the release of the ego, this light can come through to you completely unimpeded! It can blaze right through your Twin Flame womb into your living heart, where it radiates its glorious song, its life-affirming message of the omnipresent and glorious, explosive Love of God. In your heart this Love becomes God-man, God-woman, and blazes forth to amplify all My abundant Love.

So I ask you now to live this light, to love it and to see it as best you can, as it becomes free to amplify your heart. You will see, as you deeply observe through the organ of perception that is your heart, that everything in the natural world purely reflects this gold-white light to you. Then you see your heart! Nothing can ever be the same again, for your heart has been recognized as the indescribable golden-white pulsing star that is the expression of your Love.

In other words, beloved ones, now that there is no "reversal" for you, no "veil" between you and this powerful light, no inward-turning energy that made the light show up as shadows, the "Real" is present HERE, through you. You are in the world but at last, you're not of it. For certainly you understand that the Real is a vibration of the purest Love as it lives in Me, and as it nourishes all of life.

This is the purpose of "Heaven on Earth." It is to unite that which had been cut off, to return all life here to the flow of life. If this step were not necessary, the bridge not important, then all of this time I would have been saying, "You'll all be lifted up and, like the Rapture image, you'll be gone." This most certainly can happen, but not if "none be left behind."

You have understood that *"Heaven on Earth"* *means to bring the light to Earth that it may express as* *the symbols of this world.* It may express as beauty and as financial plenty and as sharing, giving, and respect. It may express as giving Love to others and seeing it multiply. It will express by becoming embedded in the symbols here of a shared world, and then be lifted slowly into pure light as everyone is ready.

Only thus, dearest ones, did we "decide" together at that moment of decision that we name the Harmonic Convergence and the LightWorkers' Decision, that to do this any other way would "burn some people up" or would leave some hearts "behind," reflecting their fears back to themselves and creating hell, not Heaven.

So, as your hearts open and clear, dearest ones, the light becomes represented in your life in the symbols of THIS world — not in the pure light of spirit. It appears in that "filmy" image that on the surface of a stream of light looks like bodies and food and work and money to represent the wealth of the spirit, the transfer of light, heart-to-heart, the transfer of the abundance of Love. It is the River of living Love in its great out-flow of giving, of sharing, caring, tenderness, of loving your brothers and sisters as your self, your Real self — expressed in the symbols here.

As this light now comes in, unimpeded, through so many hearts — and the number will increase exponentially, oh, beloved ones, we must have a way to open the rest of humanity that they also may receive this abundance and this grace.

Let Me present to you, directly to your hearts, the imprint of light that this is – that as you stay purely focused on the Real, the River of Life now comes rushing in, blazing forth light from your heart in a great explosion of gold and white. Then it radiates outward with such tenderness to set up a matrix of golden-white light, a matrix of "ley lines"— purely in spirit, radiating and connecting heart-to-heart with the people of the Earth. The great River of Life, now amplified by your Twin Flame Love, pulses through this matrix, joining all the LightWorkers together who are participating. By your intention from this seed that I planted, a living system of "life," the living "blood" of spirit, connects all hearts that at this moment are open to be drawn to this Network by radiation.

It is up to you as the bridge, dearest ones, by your focus and Love, to include all people's vibrations, so that all who need to touch My Love and My abundance can now open to accept it. Allowing the symbols of the world to gently "rest across the face of the River," you can see how this energy can be manifested here in the world. Network is the key word here — a Network of Light, a network of hearts, a network of abundance shared all together.

Your focus is what directs this energy. You can hold to the Real while you allow My Love to be funneled into this Network of Light expressed as the symbols of abundance in this world — seeing it, feeling it resonate as it calls to every life. As you hold this pattern of the Network of Light fully — as you "do the work" — you are being the bridge, the living bridge to My abundant life showing up here, accessible to all and also upholding every truth of Love and of relationship.

It is the paradigm of shared support of life force, of My abundance that can hold the vibration of the glorious Real and the vibration of pure Love. *Everything that is in your lives is for creating the Network of My living Love, manifesting freely upon the Earth in reflection of the Real.*

Dear ones, see the light, the living Now and let Me show you all its opulence, dancing, glorious shining pearls of purest light. Then you'll feel what's really happening — the opening of your hearts to the true potential life that I ever pour to you. Keep saying "yes!" *As this living light flows through your hearts and bridges the chasm, as the distance is closed between the two sides, the vibration of Earth is more and more Love.* Then the "two parts" of your lives, dear ones, will also merge as well. Trust this to occur and rejoice in this glorious Love.

The Christ child of your unions,
My beloveds,
is being born.
Just as Jesus knew
his mission had begun,
so do all of you now.
Yet yours has a glorious ending –
the awakening of
all of our beloved ones,
for they are yours
as well as Mine now.
They are the tender babes
of our heart.

The Womb of Love
Giving Birth to the Christ Light

So here we are, walking in lands of spirit that are way beyond words. You who are here are ready to give birth. This is the change that all of you are feeling, the intensity of Love, the tender cherishing of each other. The powerful urge to go forth that has been upon many of you, beloved ones, is also this. Just as in a physical birth, so is it with a spiritual one! Ah, you cannot yet see how absolutely the truth of Creation is replicated in every level of vibration. I will show you.

In a physical birth, there is the joining of the masculine and feminine that echoes exactly the process of creation. There is the womb, the ocean of Love, the "deep," hidden in the female spiral within her body, and there is the action, the male, called forth by the very thought of life itself, manifesting action born of the desire to give. (However corrupted, this is the original impetus behind physical children and, of course, behind LoveMaking. The ego has reversed this into "getting," but beneath the ego, the truth of "giving" remains).

Then does the active principle, the male, the lightning bolt going forth, come into and act upon the "ocean of the deep" that is the womb of a woman. Now Love born of the two, male and female, grows. It grows

191

until it acquires a life of its own, an energy that seeks to live — to go forth, to be Love moving forth. When this life force, the growing impetus of living Love reaches its apex, of its own accord it begins the process of birth. Signals are sent from the child to the body of the mother, the feminine. Then, dear ones, there is an opening through which new life exits the womb of its creation. The labia open and the baby's head emerges. The mother has to push, whether she likes it or not. The new life emerges into the world.

Beloved ones, I know that you are not quite able to see all these patterns and energies of creation on level after level after level. Yet you can imagine the light-filled image of the SoulMate heart, which I have also called the SoulMate or Twin Flame womb, for that is truly what it is – a place in which new life is created, gestated and brought forth. And what does the Twin Flame union look like, essentially, in energy? Very similar, indeed.

The reason I bring this forth into your awareness, beloved ones, is this. The living Love that is created by the joining of SoulMates is new life. It is an energy that is unique to the two of you. It grows and grows in each Twin Flame couple as you choose to live the heart. Such a choice – to live in the heart — is the beginning of new life, just as surely as is a fertilized egg. Also just as surely, dear ones, there comes a time for birth — a time when, of its own accord, this Love born of your union will begin to cause a push. It will be ready to go forth to be a living Love in the world – a life, not just on a physical level. Thus, rather than becoming body and personality as in the birth of a child, it becomes a force for change, for growth in Love, that is uniquely yours, the two of you.

The Love you create together, of its own accord at the level of My heart, must go forth! You are giving birth to your service together, dear ones. You are giving birth to the giving forth of Love that is a natural outcome of your SoulMate Love and your choice to live the heart. In this is your reassurance.

Dear ones, this is far beyond ego. This is the natural process of Christ Love, how it comes to be born of SoulMates, brought forth by their readiness to give Love. There is no ego in this process. You are not choosing to move forth to teach or save humanity. Rather, *Love itself now moves out through you (and you, dear ones, are along for the ride!).*

I want you to see and understand this difference. *The ego would have its own agenda. Love seeks simply to give of itself.* Dear ones, what you will do is pour forth the purest Love of which you are capable together, through your SoulMate womb, and gently bathe the others in it. This done, to the extent that they are willing, the illusion will be interrupted for them. They will see the truth — perfectly for them, and you will do this only because you are free of ego. You are so strongly in your shared heart that nothing of the illusion can capture you.

You each know the rightness of this within. You know that I speak the truth. Even if you are not able to live it every single moment yet, you are totally committed to seeing only Love. What burns within you is this desire to give Love, not because you are saviors of some sort but simply because you can do nothing else. It is true, isn't it? And should there ever be a moment where you are in getting instead of giving, you can trust yourself and/or each other to interrupt it! Ah, that is the great gift of recognizing the SoulMate. Your strength is doubled (oh, more than doubled). I can pour Love through you in far greater capacity and know it will remain uninterrupted because you hold steady for each other!

Thus, I tell you that give Love you will. *The Christ spirit rises within each of you and together with your SoulMate it will be born. It will go forth to bless and heal and lift of its own accord.* This Christ spirit, now born in and through you, heals through recognition. Oh, it is not you who do any of this, as beautiful and magnificent as you are together, you and your SoulMate. It is the Christ in you that does the work. The Christ in you, able now to pour through your SoulMate heart (womb – I use this interchangeably), unimpeded. The Christ light is the only truth of Love. Everything in it is perfect. Good. Living Love. The perfect, abundant expression of life.

As it pours through you it shows forth the truth of everything it washes in its golden light. So a person standing before you who has a seemingly broken life will see his or her life as whole. Right there, that person can accept it, and by his or her acceptance, it shall be. If they accept it, but believe it will take time, then that is exactly what will happen. If they accept it completely, they will, right there, be made completely new, and so to every degree in between.

Always one of you raises questions about your own physical bodies. My answer again is to be honest. You know that your bodies will also heal in Christ Love, perfect Love, but *there is a great service of transformation still being accomplished by LightWorkers here, now, on Earth.*

Dear ones, the laws of Love are not mitigated by your experience and that of others like you. The laws are made greater. The giving of Love is now taken to new heights by the magnificent acts of service from many of you. Yet I honor your questions, for they are valid ones. If Love is All, you ask, then why are all of you not manifesting perfection? I answer because it is important that those who serve do not become confused. *Giving Love in such great service as has been given by My LightWorkers is the greatest gift I could have been given by you, My own amazing heart.*

For some of you, the condition of your body does not seem to be following the universal law that "like attracts like," that the vibration at which you function creates your present physical plane experience, your body. Normally it does. But where the SoulMate dispensation was My gift to you, the gift of transformation was your gift to Me.*

Oh, beloveds, what an amazing gift—that you would show Me My own heart so deeply, gifting Me with the greatest gift in all the universes—offering to transmute through your bodies all that your brothers and sisters could not—that all of you shall return to Love—that every one will come to consciousness—that right now, as the Earth completes her cycle, all of you come with her. Oh, beloved ones, in this you have proven yourselves as nothing else could—sons and daughters of God, in whom I am deeply, profoundly pleased.

This is the beginning of the giving forth of Love that is now the truth of who you truly are together with your SoulMate, and thus have I now shown you the truth of this time. *The Christ child of your unions, My beloveds, is being born. Just as Jesus knew his mission had begun, so do all of you now.* Yet yours has a glorious ending — the awakening of all of our beloved ones, for they are yours as well as Mine now. They are the tender babes of our heart. They are those whom, like the Masters, you so deeply serve. You must trust that this communion of Love between you and your Twin Flame is the energy by which this Love goes forth.

Love will live you rather than you directing it, so you can always trust Me. Beloved ones, it is only by this trust that you can possibly negotiate this unfamiliar terrain of spirit. As yet you do not even have definitions of much of what we now begin together. Just remember that the experience follows your faith in its possibility, whatever expression of Love you are considering. *It is your faith in Me as all possibilities of Love that is the only thing that can take you beyond the old, known world.*

I am with you, lifting you into Heaven, right here on Earth. Every shower of golden light, every luminous, unearthly sunset is the New World peeking through—the world seen through the heart, the single eye of Love.

*This refers to the Message from God called **Transformation: The LightWorkers' Decision** (August 7, 2001). This Message is presented at the back of this book.

TO THE READER

If you have resonated strongly with what you have just read, we invite you to visit our websites,

www.circleoflight.net
www.unitingtwinflames.com.
www.netoflight.com

There you will find many Messages from God and extensive information on the Messages, Yael and Doug Powell, Circle of Light, and our Workshops to open the heart and draw the SoulMate. There are also pages on SoulMates, SoulMate Stories, Questions and Answers and a wonderful page of Sharing from the Heart from readers.

On the navigation bar, you can join our mailing list to receive the most up-to-date bi-monthly Messages from God, and if you wish, join our Tuesday Circle for transcripts of our weekly meditations. You are also welcome to communicate with us by email with any questions that arise from reading the Messages.

We particularly direct you to our new website, www.netoflight.com. At that website are Messages from God in which God has issued forth a passionate call to service to all LightWorkers, with a pathway to financial freedom that will enable us to dedicate our lives to spiritual work. "The LightWorkers are needed to return this world to Love."

On the pages that follow are two powerful personal communications given through the Messages from God. *Transformation: The LightWorkers' Decision*, referred to several times in the book you have just read, was given in August of 2001, and contains remarkable information about the offering we made to God in the depths of our hearts during Harmonic Convergence. Our pledge was that no brother or sister would be left behind in the journey Home to God, and that we would transform for those not yet "awake."

A Letter from God to Humanity on Creating a World of Love is an amazing communication that has been recorded on CD. God asked for the widest possible distribution, so we include it here. You may also obtain the recorded version free by emailing us at connect@circleoflight.net.

May you live with an open heart in a world of Love every moment!

The Team at Circle of Light

Transformation:
The LightWorkers' Decision

August 7, 2001

Every being of light in all the heavens, every being of Love in all the worlds, every wash of starlight that is embodied, every planet pregnant with life—all are holding their breath. All are holding their breath as I call you to step forth completely out of your reality and to trust that the New World will be there to place your foot upon. As I breathe in My In-breath, I feel you as the greatest Love stirring within. I too am pregnant with anticipation. In all of the worlds, all of the expanding universes, all of the trillions of beings spreading their wings of truth, there is none like you.

Now the time comes for the greatest leap of faith, faith that says that what is in your heart is the real truth, while all the structure by which you have lived your lives is an illusion. You understand this certainly, but do you understand it enough to bet your life upon it? Do you understand it enough to step forth and trust that My Love will be there? And are you ready to do this in ways both great and small, without any comparison between the world you are leaving and the world on which you arrive?

Are you willing to give up your "human home"— the ideas you have had about what it means to be a human being? Can you start with a clean slate upon which I write the truth of your life, and then you live it, moment-by-moment, step-by-step, vision-by-vision, dream-by-dream?

Dear ones, there are three very important things that have happened which have already changed your world forever. You need to understand these things deeply as you take My hand and step away from the ledge of the known world, as you step into the knowledge of your place in My heart and the truth of the "world to come." Love is "switched on" when you become a functioning cell in My heart, the heart of God, awakening.

First, in 1987, at the time of the Harmonic Convergence of energies, you made a decision in the temple of your hearts. Until that moment, there was to be a splitting of the path. Those who could make the choice for Love were to move ever higher into the light to bring forth the manifestation of humanity's evolution. The others who did not say "yes," were going to gently "drop-down" into a slower evolution, there to continue to evolve, living with those of like vibration.

At that time I felt a tugging on My heart, dear ones —a longing for those who were to be left behind. I felt keenly the emptiness within as I acknowledged that some cells of My heart would be missing, so to speak, still cloaked in illusion and darkness. You must understand that you do live within Me, and that you truly are living cells that are within My heart.

As this intense longing deepened, it became almost agonizing. Yes, I can feel agony and often have at the loss of communion with My own heart that the illusion has caused. When I looked within, I discovered something truly amazing! The longing that I was feeling was you, My LightWorkers, longing for your brothers and sisters. You did not want to leave them behind. You were My heart speaking to Me!

When I understood this, oh, My beautiful children, I fell in Love with you all over again. I understood My own heart in new ways. I knew for the first time that you truly were showing Myself to Me. You were truly opening into Love in manifestation. I knew then that all I had dreamed of for you would be true. You would be co-creators gently loving new life into being—both within you and around you. I knew that your Homecoming was going to be more than all I had dreamed. I knew that in spite of the depth of illusion into which you had fallen, you were going to emerge as something more beautiful than either of us had ever dreamed.

So, there at that moment, that juncture when so much was held in the balance, you decided together, in unison, in your hearts, on the deepest spiritual plane that you can access, that you would offer yourselves, your service and your light so that nobody would be left behind! This was the moment of My greatest joy, for you are the wild card within Me. You are the part of Me that is unknown. You surprised Me in wondrous and wonderful ways.

At that moment all beings of light who assist you, concurred. It was and is possible for the children of God, using both your Love and your Will, to lift up and clean up everything in the world, so that nothing is left behind. *In order to do this, each of you agreed that you would personally transform the darkness, limitation and illusion for those who were not able or ready to do so.* You will gladly, you told Me, offer your Love and your service for the upliftment of the whole world, of humanity and the planet into the light.

Now we are here. We are on the very real cusp of the very real awakening. LightWorkers are remembering by the thousands daily that there are real and exciting changes. But many of you are not yet remembering your agreement of service to the transformation.

The second thing that is happening, now that the changes are fully underway, is that many LightWorkers are finding themselves in unexpected situations of varying degrees of intensity— in the midst of difficult things for which there are no clear explanations. Beings of obvious light and very great Love are dealing with physical illnesses that even threaten to take them off the planet. Other beings are finding themselves in "financial crunch" though they know that I will always provide. The list goes on and on.

Many explanations are offered. These situations create fear and discomfort in those who are not so challenged. (If such a person as this who lives purely can be stricken, could this happen to me?). The ego rushes in and finds an excellent crack in the vibrations of Love, and judgment occurs. People are regularly told that they have done something to bring this on, or that they have not done their spiritual work. If all else fails, they are told that there must be some old subconscious pattern at work!

Dear ones, it is very important that you hear Me and this message of transformation. *We are now at the critical time.* One foot is on the shore of the New World and the other foot is on the shore of the Old. *Only the commitment of the LightWorkers, the pure and loving of heart, to use their lives, their bodies, hearts and Will in service to humanity's transformation will create the bridge that will bring everyone through.* To bring everyone was your promise to me. To bring everyone. Oh dear ones, this promise is how I know you are My children. All I am and more. This promise is how I know that Love will continue to show a new and more beautiful face, and that My heart will be a reflector of the pure light into the most glorious expression of our co-creation.

You must come to understand this process of transformation and this agreement. It has now become critical. If you do not, it could destroy the unity necessary to make the rise in consciousness and heart that will bring you back to The One. If you do not understand, then it will seem like chaos. It will seem that the laws of Love do not work. It will seem that the path of Love works for one person, opening them easily to obvious blessings and higher good, and does not work for another who is still suffering.

But the suffering is not their own, I tell you, My beloveds. *With the release from Time (and what you call Karma), with the extraordinary elevation in the light taking place, and with all the beings of light gathering here with you, any LightWorker choosing Love would be effortlessly rising, and everything of any negativity falling away. If that is not happening, then I guarantee you— that one is taking on the work of transformation for the rest of humanity.* This must be understood. It must be honored. It must be supported and assisted.

I ask this of all of you. In big ways or small, it is this tremendous service of doing more than your share that will bring all My children Home to Me now. And yes, ultimately all would return, but it is this extra effort that reveals your truth, your depth of Love and caring. Ultimately that will be reflected back to you in millions of ways. This too is a law of the universe, as you know.

So in this world of illusion it will be more important than ever to look very carefully at the truth of what is happen-ing. Every situation must be read with the heart. Those who are living transformers will be obvious the moment you understand the fact of this most glorious offering.

Now, let Me remind you that this agreement that all humanity would make it Home in this evolution was a concord of all of you who have light enough to understand. If you are reading this, this means you. *So I must ask you to turn right now to Me and to ask Me to show you your path of service to this transformation.* You will be amazed. You'll find things making sense that just did not make sense to you. You'll understand the "piece," as you say, about giving that is the most powerful way to your own awakening. Of course, the Love that you give holds the most powerful blessing for you of all the energy you'll receive.

Dear ones, I will guide you. Here is the third and most important thing. This fact of the LightWorkers' offering of transformation will save the Earth and allow her to rise into her own process of ascension. All of you know this is her "initiation" also, yet you have not known how to assist her. As I have told you, energy must be dealt with. The "trash" must be cleaned up. This process of transformation when combined with your conscious intent is the most powerful energy available in this universe.

Now this seems like a big thing for Me to say, until you remember who I Am and thus who you are, co-creators who are the cells of My very heart. So all beings of light everywhere are on call to your intent. I want you to absorb this. Knowing this you must now take in the fact that *nothing that is happening here is personal. If you are a being of light, conscious of Me and dedicated to Love, the forces and powers that are working in your life are universal*—dramatic rivers of light, shifts in awareness of such magnitude that you cannot yet comprehend.

So you must not "put your head in the sand!" You must not believe that this is only about you, your growth, your awakening, your ascension. THAT VISION IS FAR TOO SMALL FOR YOU. If you subscribe to such a vision, you may keep your life progressing on a steady path upward but *you would be missing out on the most amazing, dramatic and beautiful Creation story ever lived: your Creation story!* It is the story where you, My children, activate your Will, light up the cells in My heart with such power and grace that you rectify a whole evolution by redeeming what had been forced into separation and illusion —all by the power of your choice, your Love and your Will.

Dear ones, you have often heard that for this time the coming of Christ will be within you. This process of taking on transformation for the world is exactly how you will do this. Christ on the cross did exactly the same thing. He saw that humanity had fallen prey to the illusion and He transformed it by living that darkness while in the body.

It is imperative that this information be distributed and understood. If you do not know what is happening as you take on the part of the transformation you have agreed to; if you run it through your body without the understanding and the intent of the transformative light, it can be too much for the physical vehicle. We do not want the experience of your piece of the transformation to be harmful in any way. But it can be because the energies are shifting, uplifting so rapidly that you must understand transformation. You must understand it because you have agreed to do it. On some level, in some way, your piece will come to you.

The worst thing that could happen is for you or others around you to place negativity upon the experience by seeing it as something wrong with you, your clarity, your clearing, your resolution of issues, your growth in Me. Every one of those thoughts creates a negative situation where there never was one. In other words although something negative is seeming to occur, in truth it is very positive, for your intention and the intention behind the whole situation is of the most profound good. Yet one judgment from yourself or others and the purity of the offering of this service is tainted, because you are co-creators and that thought creates a very real detrimental energy.

So please, dear ones, be so very careful. Be vigilant against judgment and negative interpretation. Be especially vigilant against the assumptions and easy answers that allow you to feel better than or separate from anyone. Those are the signs that the greatest offering of humanity thus far, the assurance of their divinity by this gift reflecting My fullness in each of you, has been commandeered by the ego or the intent of separation.

When you put your foot down on the shore of the New World, what you'll find instantly is a world totally in communion and communication, first through the Internet and then through the inner knowing. *You will find a world with a unity of purpose fully engaged in the process of transformation for all—not for the individual.* This, dear ones, is the difference between the Old World and the New World.

A Letter from God to Humanity on Creating a World of Love

February 25, 2003

My beloved ones, humanity, I pour this to you with My tender Love, upon streams of light, to touch your waiting hearts. With it come the keys to your remembrance. The remembrance of your beauty and of all the ways I made you in My image. And remembrance of the truth of Love, how every human heart was born in Love and every human being is a child of God. And the remembrance that your heart is our connection and that through it lives your co-creative power. Through it comes your treasure; all the gifts I give to you forever. Through it you will now remember and find yourselves awaking to the truth of Love you are.

How I love you! You are truly the greatest of all miracles. You are My own heart, alive and in embodiment, ready to expand, to ever go forth to give the Love you are. You make Love vibrant, surprising, new. Only you, beloved ones, My precious glorious children, only you can go forth in breathless anticipation and see the Love I Am with a new perspective. Have you not marveled at your wonderful curiosity? At how insatiably you go forward to meet and greet the world?

And how deeply you are moved by every expansion of beauty? This is the miracle of your co-creative heart.

My Will for you, all of you, every sweet magnificent golden child of God, is a world of peace and a life of plenty. By looking at Me, you can have these things.

Your heart is the source of your power, your treasure, your identity, your life. Your heart is connected to Me forever. And through your heart you will receive your blessings, the treasures of joy and Love and ever greater abundance that I have waiting for you. Oh! It is My heart's true desire to deliver to you the very keys to heaven that you may live heaven here on Earth, yes, and everywhere you are for all eternity. All that is necessary is for you to return to your heart to find the joy in life that contains the heart's true resonance and the cornucopia of every good, which shall pour forth before you as your life and your world.

I Am a God of Love, dear ones. Forever and forever. There is nothing but Love in Me. Let your heart stir in its remembrance of the great truth, for on it rests the salvation of this precious world and your thousand years of peace that, truly, goes on forever. You have known this, somewhere deep inside. You have known that I Am Love and that all of this before you did not make sense. All the wars and illnesses, the brothers turning upon their brothers, the poverty, the pain, even ageing and death.

Oh, dear ones, I have heard you as you cried out in the dark night of your soul for answers. How every single one of you has asked the question, "If God loves us, why would God create children who have cancer and whole peoples who are starving; so emaciated they already look like skeletons?" It did not seem right to you. This, dear ones, was the message of your heart seeking to show you the truth. And when you have asked, "God, what is my purpose, the meaning of my life?" you have been responding to the nudging of your heart. But some, not hearing their hearts, have turned away, believing I could not be a loving parent to My children if I created such a world of horrors.

Now it is time for the truth. You are ready. And for those of you who read this and already know this, I ask you to deepen your commitment to the living of it, and to pass this on to My other precious children. For those of you who read this and find it inconceivable, I ask you to drop into a focus on your heart for a moment and just allow this to be a possibility. Then pass it on to others–that each hand, each set of eyes, each heart that comes in contact with this letter written in light may also take a moment to allow this possibility to be planted in their life.

Beloved ones, I love you. I love you with a Love as great as the very cosmos. I love you with a joy in your existence that pours forth greater in every moment. I love you as the very heart within Me. I love you, and My Love never wavers, never changes, never ever stops. I long for you to know this, to feel our sweet communion. I long to lay before you all the treasures of creation. You are Mine. Now. And Now. Forever. And nothing can ever change this. It is a fact of your existence.

I did not create this world of pain. You did. You did this when you chose to believe in good, in Love, **and** in something else, which you named the opposite of Love. Call it the moment in the Garden when you ate the fruit of good and evil. Call it the first judgment. Whatever you call it, beloved ones, it is your own creation. And you set yourselves up as being able to decide which was which and thus began this world of duality, of light *and* dark, of Love and anti-Love. But, precious humanity, I Am only Love. And living in Me, you, too, are only Love. So you had to create a false world, a pretend place where darkness could exist, because it cannot exist in that which is ever and only light, which I Am.

You have wandered in the desert of your co-creative minds ever since. For if your heart, connected to Me, knows the truth of only Love, then you had to find another way to view a dual scenario—and thus evolved the tool of your minds.

Oh, dear ones, I do not intend to go into lengthy explanations. All I come to say to you is that you are only Love. And that the more you choose to live through your heart, the more and more clearly you'll see the world as it really is. The more you will experience that true Love of God, the Love that I hold you in each and every moment.

Today you live in a world on the brink of war, a world filled with negativity and so much pain that you have to numb yourselves to survive. So you have nothing to lose by putting to the test what I now show you:

If you know that I Am only Love, then you must know that I Am ever holding for you the world of your inheritance, the world of joyous ecstasy and glorious abundance. You know that I Am not a power you can call on for overcoming darkness, for darkness is not in Me. You know that any moment you connect with Me you connect with the Love and perfection I have always held for you and always will. I Am unchanging Love. In the truth of this Love there is no negativity.

Then what about this world of pain before you? What of the wars and rumors of wars? What of the fear and all the experiences that keep happening in your life? They are you, dreaming, beloved one. They are you lost within the million threads of possibility streaming from your decision to believe in good *and* evil. And just as you dream in the night and your dreams feel real, so it is with this world. So very real and filled with pain, it feels.

There is another way to live. It is to stand before this world of lies each morning and to choose to live in only Love. To consciously reject the illusion of the judgment that there is good and evil. To place your Will in Mine and ask that I lift you up enough that you can see the difference. The difference between the truth of Love that lives within your heart and this world of swirling negativity that is alive within your mind

And once you know that I Am Love and you are ever alive in Me, then you shall truly walk through this world in peace. When you know your home is Me and you affirm the heart, you could walk through a war-torn countryside

with bombs falling all around you and know that none could
touch you, and none would touch our home.

I will answer your questions. "What about the
others?" your heart cries out. "What good is it if I am safe
in you, God, if all around me people are in misery?"
Beloved ones, the answer is this: as you clear the dream,
as you return your Will to Me, as you walk within the
truth of the Love we are together, then around you there
becomes an aura of peace; a great ball of light comes forth
as the living truth of Love you are becoming. At first it
may only clear *your* life of the illusion, as your faith in
Love restores you to the heaven you belong in, and as,
choice-by-choice and day-by-day, you turn to Me for your
identity and not to the world you have believed is outside
of you. But every day that light grows—exactly as would
happen if you turn on a physical light in a dark closet full
of scary shapes. The light fills every space—there is no
darkness left—and everything that seemed to be so
menacing becomes something neutral. Something you
can change by moving out the old furniture, or something
that you at least know is harmless.

Thus, as you grow in your ability to stay attuned
to Me, to choose the world that is your birthright as a
child of God, the greater the circumference of the light
that surrounds you. First it begins to light up your
neighbors. Suddenly they can see that there are no
terrifying things lurking in their lives; that they are free to
choose to be happy, to have joy. And with every moment
that you spend in communion with the truth of your
heart, the greater is that light of truth around you...until
you affect the neighborhood and then the town you live

in, and the county, then the state in which you live. Until ultimately you will do as Jesus did: everywhere you are, people will see their truth as Love, and knowing this with all their heart they will leave their illnesses, their problems and their strife behind—simply from experiencing the power of your light as you live your life as only Love.

Then as others do the same, soon you'll walk into the world and the illusion of negativity will have to fall away. You will have "turned on the light in the theater," that which you call the world, and all who had believed life was a battle will suddenly be freed.

In your Western world, there is a passage in the Bible from he who came to show you the way to the heart's truth: "You cannot serve both God and mammon." This is exactly what it means. You cannot believe in a world of good and evil and also seek to create a life of Love. For from within the dream of duality every choice for Love contains its opposite.

Beloved ones, if this speaks to you, if something stirs within your heart (or, of course, if you cry out, "Oh, I know this!"), then you are here to show the way. Here to see My face, My Love, in every human being, no matter the part they now play within the dream of good and evil, of Love and anti-Love. You are here to build the New, to bring forth the heaven of living Love in which you are ever meant to live. Turn to Me and daily, moment by precious moment, I will show you who you are: a child of Love so beautiful that your cloak is made of stars, your heart is a living sun lighting up the darkness and revealing only light.

Give Me your Will, let Me lift you so you can see each moment the unity of Love. How all creation is My being and every part, magnificent and joyous, dances in a swirl of sweet exploding life. I will help you see beyond duality, beyond the veil within which lives the dream of separation being dreamed by My children. I Am only Love. And your heart is the key to the treasures held for you beyond time. Time—the illusory creation coming forth from "fitting into experience" a pendulum of good and bad experience.

Beloved ones, I speak to you whose hearts have known, have known deep inside that I would not create such a world as this you see before you. It can be easy to disengage, but you've lived the illusion for a long time. Thus can you assist each other in this. Assist each other in placing your attention on your hearts and using the power of Love you find there to infuse the world you want, not the world that's passing, the world of so much pain. You are co-creators. Made in My image, remember? It is true. You are made in My image and thus do you manifest the beliefs of your heart. Remember, the heart is where we are connected, so all the power, all the light, all the Love I pour to you comes directly and unfailingly to and through your heart. I Am Creator; I Am Love expanding through you.

And My covenant with you, My children, is that I shall always and forever grant your heart's desires. This is the promise given to each of you at the moment of your creation as children of the Love I Am. So if deep in your heart you are afraid, if you believe your heart is broken (pay attention to these words), if you are afraid that Love will hurt you, if you keep yourself protected, if you are waiting every moment for "the other shoe to drop," if you feel the world is hopeless, if you feel that life's not worth it, if you feel the world's about to end, be it from polluting it to death or from chaos and war, these deep "ways you feel" about your life–these are your heart's beliefs. And thus, beloved ones, *by our covenant* they shall manifest before you. For as the Love I Am comes pouring to you, whatever is held before the opening of your heart is what Love shall bring to life, shall help you co-create.

Thus you see that, if you stand before the White House with anger in your heart, with belief that nothing changes, that government is corrupt, and, worst of all, if you hold hatred there, within the temple of God that you are, then that, dear ones, is what you shall have more of.

You are the prize of the universe–the heart of God gone forth to create. There is really only Love to create with. But if you choose Love and anti-Love, you turn your face away from Love and, peering into the world you've made, you look for your identity. Oh, precious ones, don't find it there! Please wake into the truth of Love. Place your every resource with your true and glorious heart. I promise you that Love is the only power. And that, truly, it is the heart with which you shall always create what you experience, be it now, on Earth, or later, "after death." There is no progression, no good and bad, no better and best. There is only the truth of Love or the dream of separation.

If you can make this leap, you are those who bridge heaven and Earth, who begin to reclaim the paradise you never really left. But if you cannot, then please do continue on growing in your faith in Love. It is good to pray for peace, for even though it contains the belief in its opposite, for the moments you are focusing on Love you are using your co-creative consciousness to lift you ever closer to the unity of Love. It is best, however (and I use these terms because they are relevant here), it is the true way, the way that Jesus came to show you, to see only Love. To place every bit of the power of your heart upon the paradise of Love that this Earth is in truth, giving none of your energy to the illusion that I can ever create anything but Love.

Do you see? Do you see how this must be a fantasy if in Me darkness does not exist? If I Am All That Is, which I Am, then nowhere in Creation is there anything but Love. Oh, dear ones, this I promise you. You were created in Love; made as a glorious reproduction of what I Am as Creator. You thus came forth, truly, as Twin Flames, the forces of the Divine. Ocean of Love, Divine Feminine, and the great movement of My Will upon it, Divine Masculine. Born as one with two points of conscious Love, you forever exist in a grand unity of Love, sparking together to co-create more Love.

I call you home. Home to the unity of Love I Am and that you are in Me. Every thought for peace, every prayer has value, and every act of service in Love's name to another is a star in the night of this "pocket of duality." But the real service for which many of you have come is to join together, heart after heart, in the conviction of the truth of only Love and, forming a net of your great auras of light, to lift the world free of the reversal caused by humanity's belief in good and evil.

Thank you, beloved one, for reading this. Do you feel My living presence in your heart? Do you see the light behind these words, the packages of Love I now deliver? Then you are called, beloved one. Called to remember a world of only Love. Called to place this vision before you until it sinks into your heart and becomes your one desire: to return to My children their birthright. You have angels all around you. Your hands are being held, finger of light to finger of light, by the masters who go before you to pave the way. Your every affirmation of the world of Love you choose is heralded by archangels as they trumpet across the heavens, "A child of God awakes! A child of God awakes!" And choruses of beings, living stars greater than your sun, carry forth the message that the whole of Love I Am is filled with rejoicing. For every child of God who returns heals those many lives of the dreams of anti-Love that sprang forth from their creative heart. And the whole of the cosmos is glad, because a hole in My heart, caused by your facing away into "darkness," is healed. The heart of God is mended, ah, but more than this: the Love I Am goes forth again as you to create new things for us to love together.

I Am calling. You can hear Me. It won't be long now, beloved ones.

ABOUT THE AUTHORS

Yael and Doug Powell live at Circle of Light, their spiritual center in Eureka Springs, Arkansas, that looks out over Beaver Lake and the Ozark Mountains. Both Yael and Doug are ordained ministers, and the lovely Chapel at Circle of Light is the frequent scene of beautiful sacred weddings.

Because of pain from a severe physical disability, Yael's "up-time" each day has to be carefully planned. Her priority is receiving the Messages from God in meditation and officiating at weddings. Doug is an artist and skilled craftsman at pottery, glass beads and woodworking. If it is windy, you'll definitely find him at his lifelong passion – sailing! Shanna Mac Lean, compiler and editor of the Messages, also lives at Circle of Light. If not at the computer, she can be found in the organic vegetable garden.

Completing the Circle of Light family are their wonderful animal companions. Christos (boy) and Angel (girl) are Yael and Doug's beloved Pomeranians. Ariel (Duff Duff) is a pure white cat, an older gentleman who mostly frequents the garden. Then there are the three "kitty bunnies," two-year old Rag Doll cats. Magic Cat chose this body for his current incarnation (see his book under the Say "Yes" to Love Series). Magic's Love is his beautiful SoulMate, and Sweetheart is Shanna's special darling. At Circle of Light, animals reign!

CIRCLE OF LIGHT ORDER FORM
SAY 'YES' TO LOVE SERIES

Please send the following:

____copies of *God Explains Soulmates* @ $11 _____($3 S&H)
____copies of *God Unveils SoulMate Love & Sacred Sexuality* @ $20.00
_____($3.50 S&H)
____copies of *God's Guidance to LightWorkers* @ $14 _____($3 S&H)
____copies of *God leads Humanity Toward Christ Consciousness* @ $16
_____ ($3 S&H)
____copies of *Magic Cat Explains Creation!* @ $16 _____($3 S&H)
____copies of *Giving Birth to a World of Love* @ $16 _____ ($3 S&H)

Prices are for the USA. For more than one book, reduce S&H by $1 per book or contact us. For postage to other countries, please email us first and we will find the best shipping cost.

Name:_____

Address:_____

City:_____

State:_____ Zip Code:_____

To use credit cards, please go to our web site www.circleoflight.net OR you may fax your order with credit card to (479) 253-2880.

Name on Card:_____

CC#:_____ Exp. Date:_____

If you would like to be on our email list and receive bi-monthly Messages from God, please fill out the following:

Email address:_____

Circle of Light
3969 Mundell Road, Eureka Springs, Arkansas 72631
www.circleoflight.net ♥ www.unitingtwinflames.com
connect@circleoflight.net ♥ www.netoflight.com
1-866-629-9894 Toll Free or 479-253-6832, 2774